VIRULENCE

&

INDIFFERENCE

Virulence & Indifference
A Young Polish Boy's Extraordinary Survival, Heroic Reconstruction and
Unthinkable Loss During and After World War II

Copyright © 2009 © 2013 Martin List, MD
All rights reserved.

No part of this publication may be reproduced, distributed, or
transmitted in any form or by any means, including photocopying,
recording, or other electronic or mechanical methods, or by any
information storage and retrieval system, without prior written permission
from the publisher, except for brief quotations embodied in critical
reviews and certain other noncommercial uses permitted by copyright law.
Library of Congress Cataloging-in-Publication Data is available from the
publisher.

Cover photos: Jews during Holocaust and Polish forest,
courtesy of Wikimedia Commons.

CHABAD OF NEWPORT BEACH

2865 East Coast Highway, Corona del Mar, CA 92625

ISBN: 978-0-9892404-0-6

Book design by Stacey Aaronson

Printed in the United States of America
First Edition

10 9 8 7 6 5 4 3 2 1

VIRULENCE & INDIFFERENCE

A Young Polish Boy's
Extraordinary Survival,
Heroic Reconstruction *and* Unthinkable Loss
During *and* After World War II

A Memoir

MARTIN LIST, MD

CHABAD OF NEWPORT BEACH

CONTENTS

PREFACE 1

CHAPTER ONE
Never Happen Here 3

CHAPTER TWO
Immunity Slips Away 16

CHAPTER THREE
Unsavory Compromises 28

CHAPTER FOUR
A Family Dies 39

CHAPTER FIVE
Alone 48

CHAPTER SIX
Grown-Up Child 58

CHAPTER SEVEN
Having Choices, Making Choices 67

CHAPTER EIGHT
A Brief Respite 75

CHAPTER NINE
Fighting in Palestine   95

CHAPTER TEN
Triumph at All Costs   105

CHAPTER ELEVEN
Breathing Space   115

CHAPTER TWELVE
Change of Heart   125

CHAPTER THIRTEEN
Enlightenment Beyond Education   135

CHAPTER FOURTEEN
Tremendous Buildup   147

CHAPTER FIFTEEN
Terrible Breakdown   157

AFTERWORD   165

NOTES   167

To the millions of children who were murdered ...

The loss of the contribution they would have made to civilization is beyond imagination.

PREFACE

The destruction of European Jewry was not just a matter of Germany and Hitler and the Nazis. The machinery required to round up the Jews, run the labor and death camps, dispose of the bodies, and distribute the spoils involved millions of people. You couldn't carry on a program of that scale and magnitude without tremendous support from a plethora of individuals, businesses, churches, and other organizations. Even the term *Nazi* is a whitewash, created after WWII to show that not all Germans were members of the National Socialist Party. My perspective on it is that while that may be true, all Germans—with notable exceptions dealt with in other books, articles, and movies—participated in our destruction. There was no distinction.

But not only Germans were killing us. The whole world—America, Britain, France, and all the other countries in Europe—were interacting in our destruction. Virtually every country in Europe participated in this slaughter. The French provided a volunteer SS division known as the Charlemagne division, wherein members didn't have to participate—they *volunteered* to help in the killing. English prisoners of war volunteered for the SS. The last men to defend Hitler's bunker as it was literally burning around him were volunteer Dutch SS men. Even neutral Sweden contributed an SS battalion. Germany did not do it alone.

I cannot possibly describe or even list all the horrors or incidents of Jew hating and Jew killing that have taken place over the course of my lifetime, and that continue, without apology, to this day. What I have included in these pages is truly just the tip of the iceberg. Nevertheless, this book is my tribute to the slaughtered people of my little town of Poland and, by extension, to the six million Jews who died in the Holocaust. I am the only survivor of my family, and one of just sixteen from our *shtetl* in Pilzno to survive the killing machine set in motion by Hitler, aided and abetted by both the Axis and the Allies.

It was not just a question of good people not stopping evil.

It was a matter of evil taking hold of an entire world.

Martin List, MD
Laguna Woods, CA
2007

1

NEVER HAPPEN HERE

1929-1939

My young life followed the domino pattern set in motion when Wall Street crashed on October 29, 1929, the event most historians view as the one that lifted the Nazi party out of political obscurity and subsequently paved the way to World War II. The Americans' demand for repayment of their loans, together with the swift collapse of the German export market, led to the almost overnight eradication of the German middle class—in brief, the perfect setup for Hitler's long-awaited rise to power.

I was born into that rapidly changing world landscape less than a month after the crash, on November 25, 1929, in a remote town in Poland called Pilzno, which was about one hundred twenty-two kilometers southeast of Kraków, not far from the Slovakian, Russian, and German borders. Oblivious to the goings-on of the outside world, I had a happy childhood within my family of six: my parents, Leon and Lotti, my younger sister Rosa, my older sister Nina, and my older brother Joseph. It was a loving family. My mother took tremendous care of her children—with the help of Maria, a Polish gentile who helped raise us—and was always there to give a hand to any problem.

My parents had an old-country arranged marriage. My mother didn't have much formal education, but besides being a housewife, she helped my father with their local business. A devoted, caring, loving mother, she kept a kosher home and felt it was important that my siblings and I get a Hebrew education, but she had little in common intellectually with my father, who was a powerhouse compared to her.

My father had served in the Austrian army during World War I. Afterward, he and my mother—both twenty-nine—migrated to America, where my father established a small business. They were very successful in New York, but after two years they missed their families, so they returned to their native country and started their own. My father started another business exporting groceries to Germany, and it, too, was very successful.

I remember my father had a Model-T Ford, one of only two cars in our little town. He would spend every workweek in Germany, driven back and forth by a personal chauffeur. When he came home on Saturdays, our rabbi, who lived across the street from us, would come outside and shout his displeasure about my father's violation of the Sabbath; my father would respond by shouting back. This yelling match would make my mother go bananas because she was very religious and kept the Sabbath (my father didn't have much regard for religion; he was as secular as she was religious). But while these exchanges between him and the rabbi sound volatile, they were actually often colored by humor and devoid of hostility.

Life in Pilzno before the war was rooted in community. Since the town had been part of Austria until the end of WWI, most Jews were fluent in German. In fact, Yiddish, which is nothing more than a German dialect, was really our mother tongue. And we were a small town, what is known generally in Yiddish as a *shtetl*. There were no strangers—everyone in our community knew everyone else.

Jews had lived in Pilzno as far back as 1564, when as the historical record shows, there were four Jews in town. The genealogist noted they must have been very wealthy because each of them had four servants (*sic*). In 1938, just before the outbreak of WWII, there were 1,342 Jews in our little *shtetl*, middle-class Orthodox Jews with an average of five or six children per couple, totaling about two hundred and fifty Jewish families. We were semi-autonomous from the Poles and always separate; for whatever reason, the locals were very insulted by us and never liked us. Most of my friends were Jews, but not all, and many of our neighbors were not Jews. The usual cry, if they met a boy like me, was: "Jew boy, why don't you go to Palestine where you belong?" (I wish Arafat would have heard that!) We learned to live among them, but our parents advised us to avoid discussion with them for fear of being beaten up.

We had our own schools and our own mayor of sorts, in addition to the local mayor. We also had two synagogues. Our Talmud Torah housed the *Cheder*—elementary school—across from our synagogue, as well as the local Jewish council and rabbinical court. It was a lovely wood building that accommodated a few hundred people. It also had a *shtiebl*, a little room where smaller groups could pray on weekdays.

When I was seven, I spent my afternoons studying at Talmud Torah, our Hebrew School. (Though later I was an atheist for a time, I was always a dedicated Zionist and returned to a belief in God in my later years.) In the morning we went to public school. It was one building, where we were allowed to sit on the back benches—never in the front. We may have excelled in one subject or another, but our place was always in the back seats. Unlike the gentile students, Jewish children were not allowed to sit at desks and had to hold their books on their laps. I remember studying arithmetic, reading and writing, and history. I also remember that when I entered my first grade of public school at age six, I fell in love with my teacher. I was enamored by this beautiful, Polish gentile, and she knew I was madly in love with her because I would pick flowers and wait for her with bouquets on street corners.

Whenever I could, I would bring her flowers (to the dismay of my mother because I raided every flowerbed, picking only the very best). She adored me too, partly because at a very young age I started writing Polish poetry. I must have been good at it because one day she asked if I would object to reciting some of my poetry to the director of the public schools. She beamed with pride at this little Jew boy writing Polish poetry. But I only finished third grade before the Germans decreed that Jewish children were no longer allowed to attend school.

Beyond our community and the greater town of Pilzno, I also knew a number of Germans. My parents were middle-class, small-business people who exported predominantly to Germany, so my father had many good friends there. We would visit those German families, and I would play with their children; they, in turn, would visit our home during their vacations. In winter, we would ski, ride sleds, and build snowmen together; in summer, we would swim, fish in the rivers, and play with our beautiful dog Rex. In the process, I acquired a good knowledge of the German language. The little town was like a country estate., and in summer Mondays were market days—most of the merchants were Jews who had little stalls on pushcarts. These days were always like a holiday to me because everybody was out.

My parents' house was a simple wooden structure. We had electricity installed around 1937, and we possessed one of the few telephones in the community—our phone number was 7—as well as a radio. People would come to our house whenever they needed to make a phone call or wanted to listen to a program. It was a very pleasant, happy childhood—until the summer of 1939, when I was still only nine years old.

I remember playing "bones" with one of my friends in our garden, the radio blaring in our living room. A number of our neighbors had gathered to listen to a speech by some maniac named Adolph Hitler. He was shouting at the top of his voice about how many tanks, machine guns, and planes he possessed, and how Poland must give up certain lands to him—particularly the city of Danzig and the Baltic Corridor. Inasmuch as I understood the language, I was rather shocked to hear that in the event of his being denied such claims, he would punish the enemies of Germany and destroy all the Jews of Europe, who, he proclaimed, were responsible for all the evil in the world.

My friend and I were amused by the screaming of this madman; however, as that fateful summer progressed, I learned that some from our community were not only taking him seriously, they were trying to leave Poland altogether. The problem was, no other country was willing to allow them—or any Jew—entry.

Adolph Hitler and his National Socialist German Workers'—or Nazi—Party had won an astonishing victory in the September 14, 1930 election, capturing one hundred and seven seats in the German Reichstag, the lower house of parliament. After having been considered almost a joke by many people—because the party was so small and underfunded it was close to bankruptcy—they nonetheless triumphed. In the aftermath of the Wall Street crash and Germany's subsequent economic decline, Hitler's hypnotic rhetoric played on the emotions of the Germans and won over eighteen percent of German voters. By 1931, the Nazi party was the second largest in Germany, and Hitler's autobiography, *Mein Kampf*, was heading toward making its author a millionaire.

Within three months of Hitler's appointment as Chancellor of Germany on January 30, 1933, he had leveraged trickery, thuggery, and widespread fear to acquire full dictatorial power through the Enabling Act. That same year, Dachau—the first of the Nazi concentration camps—opened to (theoretically) intern known political opponents and legally condemned criminals. Students at the University of Berlin burned thousands of books by Jewish authors, and Nazi thugs began a systematic boycott and blockage of Jewish stores and businesses. Anyone who tried to enter a German Jew's establishment to conduct business was discouraged to the point of being beaten.

But while news of the Nazi aim to make Germany *judenrein*, or cleansed of Jews, by forcing them to leave the country—which they did in droves: one in four by 1938—prompted protests and demonstrations across the United States, it did nothing to sway the Roosevelt administration or American industry, which saw profit in Hitler's warmongering.

> GM's president Alfred P. Sloan knew what was happening in Germany. Sloan and GM officials knew also that Hitler's regime was expected to wage war from the outset. Headlines, radio broadcasts, and newsreels made that fact apparent …

... Nonetheless, GM and Germany began a strategic business relationship ... Quickly, Sloan and James D. Mooney, GM's overseas chief, realized that the Reich military machine was in fact the corporation's best customer in Germany. Sales to the army yielded a greater per truck profit than civilian sales—a hefty 40 percent more. So GM preferred supplying the military, which never ceased its preparations to wage war against Europe.[1]

Furthermore, the Jews trying to flee Germany—which was simultaneously encouraged by *judenrein* policy and discouraged by emigration policy requiring payment to leave—had nowhere to go. In the summer of 1938, delegates from thirty-two countries met, at the urging of President Roosevelt, at the French resort of Evian for a nine-day conference called the Intergovernmental Committee on Refugees to discuss the problem of dealing with Jewish refugees. Roosevelt did not bother to attend or send his Secretary of State. Instead, his personal friend, Myron C. Taylor, communicated the president's concept: the US would accept Jewish refugees, but only according to an orderly, long-term quota system. Canada, Belgium, the Netherlands, New Zealand, Ireland, Britain, and Switzerland all claimed unemployment was too high to accept any refugees at all. Australia was blunter: "It will no doubt be appreciated that as we have no real racial problem, we are not desirous of importing one by encouraging any scheme of large-scale foreign migration.[2] In the end, all thirty-two governments were unwilling to take any more Jewish immigrants, a decision that amused and delighted Hitler and provided tacit support and encouragement for the German government's *judenrein* plans.

In November of that year, the British codified their endorsement of Hitler's plans to eradicate European Jews by issuing the infamous White Paper in accordance with the Palestine Mandate.

> Jewish immigration during the next five years will be at a rate which, if economic absorptive capacity permits, will bring the Jewish population up to approximately one third of the total population of the country ... some 75,000 immigrants over the next five years ... For each of the next five years a quota of 10,000 Jewish immigrants will be allowed on the understanding that a shortage one year may be added to the quotas for subsequent years, within the five year period ... In addition, **as a contribution towards the solution of the Jewish refugee problem** [emphasis added], 25,000 refugees will be admitted as soon as the High Commissioner is satisfied that adequate provision for their maintenance is ensured ... After the period of five years, no further Jewish immigration will be permitted unless the Arabs of Palestine are prepared to acquiesce in it.[3]

On May 13, 1939, nearly one thousand mostly Jewish passengers left Germany on the SS St. Louis, bound for Cuba, where they hoped to stay while awaiting visas to enter the United States in accordance with the US quota policy established at the Evian conference. Some had already experienced the horrors of the concentration camps; others sailed alone because their families could only come up with enough money for one to make the trip. They had all purchased landing permits for $150 each, allowing them to land in Cuba as tourists rather than refugees, for which a $500 bond was required according to Cuban Decree 55. But by the time the ship reached its destination, having been slowed down by a death onboard and a subsequent crew member's suicide, Cuba's parliament had passed Decree 937, nullifying those landing permits. While the St. Louis was allowed to anchor in the harbor, it could not dock at Hapag's pier, nor could the passengers disembark. It was more than a matter of money, although that was a significant piece of the equation. It was also a question of Cuban President Bru's political enmity toward Manuel Benitz, who had originally sold the landing passes, and Joseph Goebbels' well-targeted propaganda campaign that stirred up Cuban anti-Semitism with lies about the criminal nature of the passengers.

In the end, the St. Louis was forced to re-cross the Atlantic, where the passengers were transferred to other ships taking them to Holland, France, Great Britain, and Belgium. Subsequently, many fell into German hands once again.

One bright spot was American Vice-Consul Hiram (Harry) Bingham, who was posted to Marseilles, France, in 1937 and took exception to Secretary of State Cordell Hull's directive to not issue visas to Jews trying to flee Germany's *judenrein* policy. He not only granted over 2,500 visas to "Jewish and other refugees, including the artists Marc Chagall and Max Ernst and the family of the writer Thomas Mann,"[4] he went so far as to shelter some people in his own home and to help smuggle them out through the French underground. He was stopped in 1941 when an irritated American government transferred him to Lisbon.

At the end of my ninth summer, Hitler created a *causus bellum*, or justified cause for invading my country, by taking twelve Jewish prisoners from one of his forced-labor camps—either Dachau or Buchenwald—which had been operating since 1933 and 1937, respectively. After placing Polish uniforms on them and driving them to Gliwice—a town on the border between Poland and Germany, very close to where my father had his business interests—Hitler ordered them shot on the local radio station's staircase. He then brought in the entire media corps, which in those days was radio, and showed them how Polish soldiers had attacked a German radio station, informing the Nazi Reichstag that the *Wehrmacht* had been "returning fire since 5:45 a.m."[5] Such was the "legal" justification to invade Poland on September 1, 1939—an invasion that had, in reality, been underway for hours.

The Germans sliced through Poland like a knife through butter, because while the Poles were prepared with cavalry, the Germans were organized for a blitzkrieg. They came in like legions of old Rome—unconquerable, frightening. The far-superior mechanized German army had no trouble defeating the Polish army in a matter of days. When the first truckload of Germans rolled into my little town around mid-September, my mother and I were peeking through the curtains, and we heard them burst out in song with lyrics that said: "The Jewish blood spurts from our knives."

I turned to my mother. "Why do they want Jewish blood?"

"Be quiet," she said. "We were here in 1914. The Germans are a civilized nation. They're not going to do us any harm. It's just a war."

That was part of the tragedy. No one really thought the German culture could produce this kind of terror. In fact, many of the men in our town had already run away because no one thought the Germans would do anything to women or children. My uncle

—my father's brother—did exactly that: he left his wife and two children and fled to Russia. A quarter of a million people ran away to Russia or eastern Poland, and as a result, fell into Russian hands when the Nazis and Soviets divided up the country in the German-Soviet Boundary and Friendship Treaty of September 28, 1939. Afterward, Stalin put out a referendum: "Given a choice, would you Jews want to go back to where you came from in German-occupied Poland or stay where you are?" Ninety-seven percent said they would like to go back to German-occupied Poland. So Stalin, in his paranoia of everything, shipped them all off deep into Siberia and Mongolia and such places where, fortunate for them, they survived. However, they did not survive under German occupation. In my definition, those who went to Siberia were refugees, not survivors, but many of them were neither. I found out after the war, for example, that my uncle died fighting the Germans, while his wife and children were sent to Belzec.

My family was left behind with the other wives and children, but not because my father had run away. He had been inducted into the Polish army in August due to his previous military experience in WWI.

I did not start school that September. The Germans decreed that Jewish children could no longer go to public school, and I couldn't go to the Hebrew school anymore because that very week they burned it down, together with our temple. I was devastated because I loved school, but of course we believed it was temporary. It wasn't.

We lived not far away from the synagogue, and as the fires spread, we—my mother, brother and sisters, and our tenant, a young Jewish lady who had married three months earlier and whose husband had run away to Russia—stood outside and watched. A German dressed in an SS uniform—the very Hollywood image of a Nazi—stood watching as well, trying to console us that the fire would not reach our home. I remember he already had information on everybody. While the fires were burning the synagogue, he turned to our tenant and said, "You have a bicycle store, don't you?"

"Yes."

"Good," he said. "I'll come by tomorrow and pick a bike." And he did. He came and picked out the best bicycle in the store, never as much as mentioned paying for it, and rode off.

At the same time they burned down our synagogue and schools, they immediately issued orders, all of which were signed by the German general in charge, whose name ironically was List—my name. It was kind of funny to me to read the placards they were putting on the walls: If you don't do A, B, C, or D, you're going to be shot. Signed, General List.

The signs declared that all Jews were prohibited from practicing any profession, and that they must give up any radio sets, weapons, foreign currency, gold, or securities in foreign banks. In addition, it was decreed that we wear an armband with the Star of David. All of these held the consequence of death if we didn't comply.

Meanwhile, my father had run away from the disintegrating Polish army and was, like so many others, fleeing eastward toward Russia. He never quite reached the border, however. He showed up one day at home wearing civilian clothes. As he embraced my mother, he said, "It's a miracle I'm alive. One morning I was shaving in the army with this little mirror in front of me. A Polish officer—a gentile—immediately accused me of being a spy for the

Germans. He said I was using the mirror to send signals to German airplanes!"

My father was immediately court-martialed, sentenced to die, and sent to a nearby forest where he escaped, just before being shot.

Interestingly enough, once the Germans took over our town, the local Gestapo started searching for him—my father, specifically—because they knew he had connections in Germany. One of us children would always be on the lookout for the Gestapo approaching our house. At least once a week, they would drive up and break in like gangsters. "Where is he? Where is he?" they shouted. But as we always saw them approaching, my father would go out the back door and escape. So he was persecuted first by the Poles for supposedly helping the Germans, and then by the Germans for being a Jew with close German relations.

2

IMMUNITY SLIPS AWAY

1940-1942

Periodically, even before Hitler devised his "Final Solution," the Germans would take some member of our community every few days and simply shoot him, just for the fun of it, to invoke fear and exercise control over us. Life under these conditions became virtually unbearable. My mother, who was very orthodox, believed the rabbi when he said this was all "God's Will," just another test for the Jewish people to prove their faithfulness to the Torah's six hundred and thirteen commandments. My father the atheist wanted to take us all into the Soviet Union, the border of which was one hundred and twenty miles, or two hundred kilometers, east. But my mother would have none of it. "It will all pass soon," she kept repeating.

Fortunately, my father had a back-up plan. He had prearranged for the Hurkovas, former business associates, to "Aryanize" our home. Our house was fairly large and easily separated into two equal parts, or apartments, linked by a door that could be closed at will. They moved into one half sometime in January 1940; we confined ourselves to the other half. To all appearances, the house was now occupied by Germans. The agreement was for them to take over our possessions, protect our assets, and return them as

Immunity Slips Away

the need arose. Mr. Hurkova actually hated Jews, but he got along with my father because of their business dealings and, perhaps, because my father was an atheist. Mrs. Hurkova was friendlier; like my mother, she did not believe Hitler really meant to harm the Jews.

The Hurkovas had two daughters and a son, Walter, who in April 1940 volunteered for the Waffen SS that was stationed in France. Their older daughter, Trudy, was married to Alois, who, like his father-in-law, was an alcoholic with a profound hatred of Jews. Their younger daughter, Ursula, was about my older brother Jozef's age. He picked flowers for her and took her on long bicycle rides during the nice weather, and ice skating and on sled rides during the winter. For awhile at least, they shared a mutual infatuation.

Besides the Hurkovas, we had many other German friends, some of whom were conscripted into the German army, and our home was their home while they were stationed in Poland. My parents threw nonstop parties on weekends in our beautiful gardens. The German friends loved smoked Polish ham, which was rationed in Germany, so we provided them all the ham they wanted. They, in turn, brought us bags of saccharine, which was readily available and even cheap in Germany. With sugar and saccharine unobtainable in Poland, we traded saccharine to the Poles for food and other comforts. Each pill was like gold.

After the Germans defeated the French, even my parents' friends took on the arrogance of the other German soldiers in town, constantly bragging they were destined to rule the world. Many were veterans of conquering France and loved to show off photos of themselves next to the Eiffel Tower and the Arc de Triomphe in Paris. Their cockiness was indescribable; they were like Roman Centurions. I overheard a number of discussions during those weekend parties about other German friends receiving notice of their loved ones—political enemies of the regime—dying from heart attacks in a place called Auschwitz. They were somewhat surprised so many were succumbing to the same disease. Soon everyone came to know the name "Auschwitz." That's where the Polish clergy were being sent to eliminate any intelligentsia resistance to Nazi rule.

Our community had always had a Jewish council and rabbinical court in the Talmud Torah across from the synagogue until the Germans burned it down. Now, they created instead a "Judenrat," a sort of Jewish community council to serve the occupiers. Gestapo officers would regularly arrive at the Judenrat and demand a list of twenty people to be shot. The Judenrat leaders tried desperately to avoid providing young people for this devilish purpose, so they picked only the old, feeble, and crippled. It was a hellish task. One of the Judenrat leaders, Hershel Bochner, was a friend of my father's who became instrumental in helping my family survive for as long as it did.

Even without the Judenrat list, no one was really safe. The Germans' special forces would drive around our little *shtetl* on bicycles and target a Jew here, a Jew there, shooting them on the street like they were dogs, without any reason. The SS and Gestapo would round up young Jews for road construction and heavy labor by merely choosing people off the street or raiding their homes. In the process, these victims were always subject to severe beatings. The whole purpose was to demoralize our entire community—and it worked.

The German soldiers also greatly enjoyed having fun with us. One day a few grabbed my grandfather, a religious Jew with a full beard, handed him a broom, and ordered him to sweep the streets while they took photographs to send home. Then, bracketing him between them, they struck a match and incinerated his beard. This caused hysterical laughter. The local population equally enjoyed the spectacle. That evening, my grandfather said, "I don't understand this world anymore. I used to know Germans in WWI. They were not like these Germans. They were civilized people. I no longer know what's going on."

That night, he hanged himself.

I have to believe that my grandfather's suicide, the incidents in town, and our German friends' repeated warnings of what was coming for the Jews must have prompted numerous discussions between my parents to which I was not privy, but I do know my mother stood firm: she would not go to Russia. My father did not want to split up the family, so we stayed and, like all the rest of the Jews around us—even the rabbi—kept a low profile.

Life went on somehow. I continued to be tutored by my Hebrew teacher, but no other studies were available to me. I did manage to get books from the local library, but only on the sly, because that too was forbidden for Jews. I instead devoured German newspapers, which gave me an early political education. I particularly enjoyed reading *Der Sturmer*, the most virulent anti-Jewish paper in all history. It was published by prominent Nazi Julius Streicher, who was convicted of crimes against humanity and executed in Nuremberg. Today's Arab press reminds me of that publication, which was a central element of the Nazi propaganda machine. When I wasn't reading, I rode my bicycle and played soccer with my Polish friends—always on opposite teams, of course. Life was difficult, but my mother reassured me things would all soon revert to normal.

The German army took over most of Western Europe and Scandinavia in 1940 (except for Sweden, which continued supplying the German war machine with iron and steel). Early in 1941, orders were issued forbidding the use of any public or private road by anyone except the German military. Between February and June, a mass of German military personnel poured toward Russia, in clear violation of the Molotov-Ribbentrop Treaty Hitler had signed with Stalin before he attacked Poland. Belgian horses and tanks the size of cottages pulled long artillery and other guns. Armed vehicles and thousands of brand new French military trucks constituted a steady parade eastward toward the nearby Soviet border. It was heartbreaking to see all those German battalions in trucks the French didn't bother to destroy before handing them all over to the conquering Germans.

The sheer volume of armor—tanks, trucks, mechanized units, horse-drawn artillery, overhead Messerschmitt planes covering the skies—was so vast I could not imagine anyone or anything defeating it. Clearly, nothing in the world could stop the Germans from taking over the whole world. I remember my father asking one of his German friends, a senior officer, the meaning of it all. He answered with a proud smile: "We expect to be in Moscow in fourteen days, then no more Soviet Union!"

Not one of that sea of men and armor ever returned.

The Germans took hundreds of thousands of Russian prisoners of war. Once, I witnessed a convoy of trucks transporting Soviet POWs. The convoy stopped at the roadside so the captors could have their lunch. There were no provisions for the prisoners. A downpour began, and some of the prisoners stuck their hands out to catch a few drops of rain. The German soldiers —ordinary conscripts, some no more than eighteen or nineteen years old—ran around the trucks bayoneting their palms. No water for the starving prisoners!

As the Germans took more and more of Russia, we heard stories of mass murders of Jews by the *Einsatzgruppen*, the SS's special "mobile killing units," who poured into the German-conquered territories. They said: "Jews were rounded up in every village, transported to a wooded area or a ravine (either natural or constructed by Jewish labor). They (men, women and children) were stripped, shot and buried."[6] The *Einsatzgruppen* shot one hundred and twenty thousand Jews in one day at a Ukrainian ravine near Kiev called Babi Yar, an incident immortalized in a poem by Yuri Yevtuchenko. Local Russians observed that many of the people in that massive grave in Babi Yar were still alive; the earth heaved and writhed for almost two days as some fought their way out from among the corpses, while others choked to death.

Babi Yar

No monument stands over Babi Yar.
A steep cliff only, like the rudest headstone.
I am afraid.
Today, I am as old
As the entire Jewish race itself.

I see myself an ancient Israelite.
I wander o'er the roads of ancient Egypt
And here, upon the cross, I perish, tortured
And even now, I bear the marks of nails.

It seems to me that Dreyfus is myself.
The Philistines betrayed me – and now judge.

I'm in a cage. Surrounded and trapped,
I'm persecuted, spat on, slandered, and
The dainty dollies in their Brussels frills
Squeal, as they stab umbrellas at my face.

I see myself a boy in Belostok.
Blood spills, and runs upon the floors,
The chiefs of bar and pub rage unimpeded
And reek of vodka and of onion, half and half.

I'm thrown back by a boot, I have no strength left,
In vain I beg the rabble of pogrom,
To jeers of "Kill the Jews, and save our Russia!"
My mother's being beaten by a clerk.

O, Russia of my heart, I know that you
Are international, by inner nature.
But often those whose hands are steeped in filth
Abused your purest name, in name of hatred.

I know the kindness of my native land.
How vile, that without the slightest quiver
The anti-Semites have proclaimed themselves
The "Union of the Russian People!"

It seems to me that I am Anna Frank,
Transparent, as the thinnest branch in April,
And I'm in love, and have no need of phrases,
But only that we gaze into each other's eyes.
How little one can see, or even sense!
Leaves are forbidden, so is sky,

Immunity Slips Away

But much is still allowed – very gently
In darkened rooms each other to embrace.

"They come!"

"No, fear not – those are sounds
Of spring itself. She's coming soon.
Quickly, your lips!"

"They break the door!"

"No, river ice is breaking…"

Wild grasses rustle over Babi Yar,
The trees look sternly, as if passing judgement.
Here, silently, all screams, and, hat in hand,
I feel my hair changing shade to gray.

And I myself, like one long soundless scream
Above the thousands of thousands interred,
I'm every old man executed here,
As I am every child murdered here.

No fiber of my body will forget this.
May "Internationale" thunder and ring.
When, for all time, is buried and forgotten
The last of anti-Semites on this earth.

There is no Jewish blood that's blood of mine,
But, hated with a passion that's corrosive
Am I by anti-Semites like a Jew.
And that is why I call myself a Russian![7]

On January 20, 1942, the Nazi high command and the leaders of the SS—no less than a dozen with PhDs—got together at the Wannsee Villa in Berlin to eat hors d'oeuvres served by waiters in coattails and bow ties, drink cognac, and hear Adolph Eichmann describe how to carry out what was now a strategic imperative of the Third Reich: the "Final Solution of the Jewish Question." Of course, we did not know anything about it at the time, but that conference sealed my family's doom.

That July, the Germans put up notices all over town instructing all the Jews to leave their homes and report to a narrow section of our town, right across the street from where we lived. Our rabbi again told us this was God's will, so despite my father's protests, we took what we could in bundles on our backs and crossed the street. The Germans immediately put up a fence of barbed wire around the entire area. Though it was five feet high, one could easily lift it and slip under and out. But no one did. Instead, all two hundred plus families remained in the Ghetto area in mostly Jewish houses, five families to one little place, ten people to a room. A strict rationing system was instituted, whereby we received only a hundred and eighty grams of bread a day per person. This, we all had come to know, had become standard procedure all over Poland at the time. Our former home was now completely taken over by the Hurkovas.

After four weeks, on August 18, 1942, the Gestapo ordered all Ghetto inhabitants to assemble in the town square, which was inside the Ghetto. They had a document from the Judenrat that listed all the families. They read off each name. Everyone was present, except one family: the Lists.

Immunity Slips Away

We had been summoned that day from our ghetto quarters by the Germans, but upon arriving in the square and observing the chaos, my father proclaimed that he had had enough. "You can go with God's will," he told my mother as she vehemently objected, "but I'm taking the children out." Without being noticed, amidst the mayhem, he lifted up the barbed wire, herded us all through, and led us across the street to our former house. As the Gestapo separated the rest of our town into three sets of trucks and wagons —the strong to go to Dembitz, a nearby labor camp; the pretty young girls to be taken to the House of Soldiers down the road; and the rest to be transported, *they believed*, to work in Russia—we hid in the basement of our own house, with Mrs. Hurkova's knowledge and permission. Meanwhile, the Gestapo took the time to shoot a few people, as if to set an example, beat some who protested, and set ferocious dogs on others.

They should have known at that moment they were all going to die.

As the Germans categorized everyone for trucks, labor camps, etc., they discovered that the List family was absent. They knew we had a special relationship with the family who was living in our house, so a few officers immediately drove to it and asked Mrs. Hurkova of our whereabouts. She denied knowing anything. They insisted on searching the house and warned her of the dire consequences of helping Jews. From our hiding spot in the basement, we could hear every word they said.

"Look, you are German. You know very well that helping Jews means that if we find them here, we have to kill you. But if you show us where they are, we won't hurt you."

She laughed. "You must be crazy. I'm a German woman. Why would I do this for Jews? Let me make lunch for you. Sit down. We'll finish lunch and then you can go and look."

I don't know what she hoped to achieve; she knew we were there. After lunch the Germans would search, find us, and either arrest her or shoot her on the spot.

Meanwhile, a certain Ludwig Baczek had been in the town square during the reading of the names and noticed that we didn't answer when our names were called. Baczek was a known criminal, but his wife was a friend of Mrs. Hurkova's so he knew the layout of our house. He had no great love for Jews, but he hated authority and derived special pleasure from defying it at every turn. He, too, concluded we must be hiding in our former house, and proceeded to steal a German military vehicle, park in the back of the house while the Gestapo was having lunch in the front, and head straight for the basement.

"Psst, psst—come out!" he called. We all came out and followed him to his stolen truck, which was parked right behind a jeep where the Gestapo stood.

"What are you doing?" a Gestapo agent called to him. "Are those Jews?"

"How dare you insinuate that I'm hiding Jews!" Baczek said. "I'm German, like you!" And with that he drove us away, with the Gestapo in hot pursuit. But he knew the little roads and they didn't. He lost the Germans, and took us to a forest.

When we got to the forest edge and everyone got off the truck, Baczek gave what I call his Lincoln speech. "List," he said, addressing my father, "you are all going to die. This war is going to last a long time, and none of you is going to make it. Take it from me; I've been a criminal all my life. I know what I'm talking about.

But I'll make you a generous offer, do you a favor. I have a hammer here. I'll kill your entire family with this hammer right now so the Germans don't get them, and I'll help you survive the war."

My father was obviously shocked. He said, "Look, you're a wonderful man. I don't know how to thank you. What you did was very brave. But please don't kill my family. We'll take our chances in the forest."

With that, my father offered Baczek clothes, possessions, even gold, but the criminal said, "No, I don't need gold. Keep it. You'll need it; I won't." He gave us all a few pieces of advice on how to survive, climbed back into his stolen truck, and left us in the forest.

Alive.

3

UNSAVORY COMPROMISES

1942

That first day in the forest was paradise. I felt free like a bird, and figured I was going to survive no matter what. Other people eventually showed up, but for the first two months, we were alone.

My father led us deep into the woods, far away from the road. My mother did nothing to help at first—she kept moaning about defying the will of God—but my father said, "Let's start building a bunker" and got us focused on living. He had military experience from World Wars I and II, so he had the knowledge to build what we needed. What he didn't have was tools.

We couldn't risk going back to get them from our former home at that point, but we used broken tree branches and our bare fingers. I had a little penknife too, with about an inch-long blade to dig the bunker. It took two days, but we made the hole just big enough to hold us all when we were in the fetal position. It was a ditch, but we were dry in it. The problem was what to do with the dirt. Our only option was to carry it at nighttime as far as we could and spread it around. It was a horrendous task performed with great difficulty. But we knew that people would come into the forest, and if they found any signs of our being there they would call the SS or the Polish police—or worse, simply kill us on the spot. We used branches to cover up the hole, then put twigs and leaves on top of the branches. It looked perfectly natural. You could come to within a yard of it and you wouldn't know we were there.

Of course, there were no bathroom facilities. Everyone knew they had to go as far away from the bunker as possible. We used dead trees as "bathrooms" and were always careful to cover our waste with leaves so people wouldn't see it and become suspicious. Of course, animals would get into it, but we could not stop that. Still, no one was likely to stumble upon us, even though people came into the forest all the time to collect firewood and to pick the abundant mushrooms, blueberries, and raspberries. I lived on those foodstuffs for a long time.

People also came into the forest to set traps for rabbits. It was horrible. The poor rabbits would try to bite off their own leg to get free. We occasionally stole them out of the traps, built a fire out in a field, and ate them ourselves. Between the mushrooms, berries, and rabbits, we did not go hungry. We also stole potatoes from the fields, as well as turnips and pears. But except for those occasional rabbits, we had no protein. Water was a huge problem too. We were always thirsty and could only go at night to a nearby river, about four kilometers—or two miles—from the bunker. We stole watering cans from the Polish farmers whose crops we were also stealing and didn't think twice about it. Those Poles wanted to kill us; we felt justified in taking whatever we needed to stay alive.

After a while, we got used to life in the forest. The only one who lamented was my mother. I don't mean to criticize her; she loved us dearly and was a very caring person. She did everything for us, more than any mother I have ever seen, then or since. But she was very protective, maybe even overly protective. In 1939, before Hitler invaded Poland, Nina had wanted to go to the World's Fair in New York. If she had been there as a tourist when the war broke out, my mother's family—who had all stayed in New York—would probably have insisted she stay in America with them. But my mother, with her best protective maternal intentions, objected to her daughter traveling alone to such a distant country, so Nina stayed in Poland with the rest of us and shared our fate.

Because of my mother's strict religious beliefs, she accepted our rabbi's view that our lives—all Jews' lives—were controlled by God's Will. Allowing ourselves to be herded into the ghetto was God's Will. Going along with whatever the Germans wanted us to do, wherever they wanted us to go, was all God's Will. All the people in our community believed the same thing. In fact, most of the European Jews, who were all very religious, believed the Jews' fate, whatever it might be—pogroms, ghettos, labor camps, gas chambers—was God's Will.

My father was an atheist. Before long, so was I.

While we dug and scrabbled in the dirt, the bulk of our community —those not sent to work in one of the Dembitz slave factories or to be prostitutes at the local House of Soldiers—were taken by horse-drawn wagons and trucks to Debica, where they were packed like sardines into railroad wagons and transported to an extermination camp known as Belzec. The journey from Debica to Belzec took a few hours. The train left in the late evening and collected Jewish people from neighboring communities along the

Unsavory Compromises

way. That was the last I heard of my community—all those beautiful children I grew up with, my Hebrew teachers, and my extended family of cousins, aunts, and uncles.

By pure coincidence, I came across an article some fifty-nine years later about an SS officer named Kurt Gerstein—a German disinfection officer attached to the Hygiene Institute of the Waffen SS—who witnessed the executions at Belzec on the very day my community was transported to that death center. I was not there, but his official report relates the truth far better than I ever could.

> The first train arrived after some minutes from the direction of Lemberg. Forty-five wagons with 6,700 people of whom 1,450 were already dead on arrival. Behind the barred hatches children as well as men and women looked out, terribly pale and nervous, their eyes full of the fear of death. The train comes in: 200 Ukrainians fling open the doors and whip the people out of the wagons with their leather whips. A large loudspeaker gives the further orders: "Undress completely, also remove artificial limbs, spectacles etc …"

> Then the procession starts moving … Mothers with babies at their breast, they come onward, hesitate, enter the death chambers! At the corner a strong SS man stands who, with a voice like a pastor, says to the poor people: "There is not the least chance that something will happen to you! You must only take a deep breath in the chamber, that widens the lungs; this inhalation is necessary because of all the illnesses and epidemics …"

> Many people pray. I pray with them, I press myself in a corner and shout loudly to my and their God. How gladly I would have

entered the chamber together with them, how gladly I would have died the same death as them. Then they would have found a uniformed SS man in their chambers—the case would have been understood and treated as an accident, one man quietly missing. Still I am not allowed to do this. First I must tell what I am experiencing here!

The chambers fill. "Pack well!" ... the people stand on each other's feet. 700-800 on 25 square meters, in 45 cubic meters! The SS physically squeezes them together, as far as is possible.

The doors close ... The people are brought to death with the diesel exhaust fumes. But the diesel doesn't work! ... I wait. My stopwatch has honestly registered everything. 50 minutes, 70 minutes [?]—the diesel doesn't start! The people are waiting in their gas chambers ... After two hours and 49 minutes—the stopwatch has registered everything well—the diesel starts. Until this moment the people live in these 4 chambers, four times 750 people in 4 times 45 cubic meters! Again 25 minutes pass. Right, many are dead now. One can see that through the small window in which the electric light illuminates the chambers for a moment. After 28 minutes only a few are still alive. Finally, after 32 minutes, everyone is dead!

From the other side men from the work command open the wooden doors. They have been promised—even Jews—freedom, and some one-thousandth of all valuables found, for their terrible service. Like basalt pillars the dead stand inside, pressed together in the chambers. In any event there was no space to fall down or even bend forward. Even in death one can still tell the families. They still hold hands, tensed in death, so that one can barely tear them apart in order to empty the chamber for the next batch. The corpses are thrown out, wet from sweat and urine, soiled by excrement, menstrual blood on their legs. Children's corpses fly through the air. There is no time. The riding crops of the Ukrainians lash down on the work commands. Two dozen dentists open mouths with hooks and look for gold. Gold to the left, without gold to the right. Other dentists break gold teeth and crowns out of jaws with pliers and hammers.[8]

Gerstein reported his experiences to the secretary of the Swedish legislation in Berlin, and discovered later it had "considerable influence on Swedish-German relations." He could not, however, get it to the Holy See, despite trying to report to the Papal Nuncio in Berlin and even speaking to the company lawyer of the Catholic Bishop of Berlin. As with the March 1942 appeal letter sent by the leaders of the entire Slovakian Jewish community to beg the Pope's intercession on their behalf, Gerstein's pleas for Vatican help and intervention fell on deaf ears.

My extended family was gone. I learned later that my father's brothers and their families had been exterminated at Belzec, some by gas, and some by other means. My Uncle Moses—who, like my father, had been conscripted into the Polish army in 1939—eventually joined the Soviet army and was killed by the German invading force. His wife and children were gassed in Belzec while we were still in the ghetto.

Uncle Fishel's family found its way into the forests but was discovered by the Polish police. The entire family was killed except for my two cousins, Mendel and Herschel, both of whom survived the war in the forests as I did, only to be dragged out of bed after the liberation by the A.K. (home army), whose sole purpose was to kill any surviving Jews. They shot Herschel; thankfully, Mendel escaped and eventually reached the United States.

Uncle Joseph and his family also hid in another part of the forest, but they too were betrayed by Polish farmers. When the Polish police arrived in short order, Joseph tried to defend his family with an ax, but the police smashed in their skulls with their rifle butts. Joseph's thirteen-year-old daughter Sarah somehow managed to escape in the chaos and tried to reach our part of the forest. Unfortunately, she succeeded in making contact instead with Ludwig Baczek. He proceeded to rape and kill her with that same hammer he'd offered to use on everyone but my father. He dumped her body in a ravine, where she was identified by the authorities.

Following my liberation, I approached Baczek and asked why he had committed this atrocious act. Without denying any of it, he merely reminded me that I had no right to complain; if not for his brazen act on the day the Germans dissolved our ghetto, I would not be alive today. At a loss for words, I burst out crying.

By fall, my sister Nina could no longer cope with life in the forest. She was a few years older than I, and like our parents and brother she was quite tall, making it very difficult for her to be in the bunker. She was an outgoing person with dreams of traveling, and we were virtually confined to living in a hole in the ground all day, coming out only at night to relieve ourselves and forage for food and water. Nina simply could not take sitting there day after day thinking about what the Germans or Poles would do to her if we were found. The possibilities terrified her. She begged our father to obtain potassium cyanide so she could commit suicide rather than endure a brutal death at their hands.

I understood her terror. In fact, none of us expected to survive. I, too, constantly thought about being captured and tried to imagine what being shot would feel like. Unfortunately, one could only obtain potassium cyanide from an apothecary, where they knew very well that even if it was Mrs. Hurkova who came in to buy such pills, it would have to be on behalf of Jews, and that would mean instant death to all of us, including Mrs. Hurkova. Consequently, my father discarded the cyanide idea, and instead decided to try to get Nina a working permit in one of the Dembitz ghetto's slave factories, where those selected from our town for labor still remained. At nineteen, Nina was strong and very beautiful, with dark hair and much nobility in her demeanor. I loved her very much and we got along well. If we had stayed through the sorting, she probably would have been sent to Dembitz or to the House of Soldiers. Either, as far as she was concerned, was preferable to life in the bunker.

At one point, my father sneaked out of the forest and made contact with Mrs. Hurkova, who in turn made contact with Hershel Bochner, the head of the Dembitz Judenrat. The Judenrat served the Germans, but they were not unreasonable people. They'd been picked to do the dirty work because the Germans did not want to do it themselves and enjoyed making Jews turn against each other.

Bochner agreed to provide the necessary papers for Nina, and because he knew he would be forewarned when the Dembitz labor places were going to be liquidated and their inhabitants sent to the gas chamber, he would let my father know. In return, my father had to guarantee that when Bochner sent out the signal, we would arrange for him to get out of there and transport him in secrecy to the forest.

So Nina was smuggled into one of the slave factories and remained there for about three months. While she was gone, the number of people hiding in the forest increased. One of the new occupants was Wolf Einspruch, a strapping young man who had escaped from a cattle car on the way to Auschwitz. The top of the car had a small window crisscrossed with barbed wire. Wolf managed to break the barbed wire and slip through the opening, jumping from the moving train with a hail of bullets directed at him from machine-gun positions on the top of every third car. He broke his arm as he hit the ground, but still managed to get away.

Wolf's arm had become infected by the time he made contact with us in the forest and was actually starting to rot away. We took him in the middle of the night to a local Polish doctor a few miles away. He, of course, rejected our pleas for help and threatened to call the police. We in turn told him that Wolf was going to stay with him until he fixed his arm and that we would hold his little daughter as a guarantee. With that, we took his nine-year-old daughter to the forest while he treated Wolf. After about ten days, Wolf's arm had healed and we returned the doctor's daughter.

Wolf looked like a movie star, very well built, good looking, and powerful. By then we had a number of young women in their early twenties and late teens in our group in those bunkers. Because we all knew we were going to die, the women felt no shame having sexual intercourse with Wolf every time they felt like it, in front of everyone. It was like, "Live for today, die tomorrow." Although I was only in my early teens, I sensed this very strongly. Sexuality was very open among those of us who were going to die, the general attitude being: *Do whatever you want*.

My brother Jozef felt the same way. He would sneak back to see Ursula every chance he got. Whenever he went back to our former house, we always begged him not to tell her where we were. "Just say you are hiding somewhere. Please, please don't tell her where!" we pleaded.

Around Christmas, Ursula's brother Walter came home unexpectedly and walked in on her and Jozef. He immediately pulled his revolver to kill Jozef and was going to kill his own sister as well for helping a Jew, but Mrs. Hurkova intervened. "Walter, remember, the law says that if anyone is caught helping a Jew, the whole family will be shot, which means me, your father, your sister and her husband, and even you, Walter." So he left them alone and Jozef escaped back to the forest.

Not long after, Bochner signaled us of the Dembitz ghetto's pending liquidation. We took Nina back to Mrs. Hurkova, who again risked her life for her. Even in the face of the sacrifices she made, I had and still have very mixed feelings about Mrs. Hurkova. While there was understandable resentment that she was well paid for everything she did and ended up with our house and everything we owned, we couldn't deny that she took enormous, repeated risks to help us. She got Nina back to us, and she also helped us get Bochner and his family out, as we had promised. Again, my father gave her gold, but as she was risking certain death, I supposed she deserved it. Although Bochner did not join us in the forest, he managed to hide his entire family. Most of them survived, including him, and they eventually found their way to the United States.

When Nina came back to the forest from the slave factory, she had changed. There was heightened fear in her and she was almost obsessed with procuring cyanide. I don't know exactly what she went through while she was away, but whatever it was she came back afraid and without hope.

Nina was accompanied by a sixteen-year-old girl from a wealthy Jewish family from Hamburg, Germany. Bochner had somehow managed to persuade Mrs. Hurkova to take her, along with my sister. The girl was totally lost; she could not speak a word of Polish, and her parents had obviously already been killed. Though she was very beautiful and delicate, I am sure Mrs. Hurkova did not save her out of love for us or anyone else; either Bochner or my father paid her for the girl. But again, had she been caught, even by her anti-Semitic husband or son-in-law, she would have been instantly arrested and shot.

We took the girl—I can no longer remember her name—under our wing and brought her to live with us in a bunker in the forest.

4

A FAMILY DIES

1943

The winter of 1942-43 was particularly cold in the forests of Poland. The German army had just experienced their worst defeat on the Russian front, which somehow translated for them into an even more furious need to exterminate every possible Jew. To make matters worse, Mrs. Hurkova grew continually more reluctant to return to us any of the funds my father had entrusted to her. Consequently, food became increasingly more difficult to obtain through those long, cold months. Fortunately, because the sun came up late and went down early, we had more time to scavenge and steal. It was a slow process; every time we took one step, we had to cover the preceding footprint.

We occasionally utilized certain survival tips from Baczek. He had shown us, for example, how to grab a dog's tongue if he was trying to bite you, and he told us how to use our fingers to poke a person's eyes if we were caught, which would give us time to get away. He also told us how we could kill someone by stabbing a long needle into the spleen on the left side of the abdomen, but I never had a long needle and, fortunately, never had occasion to have to defend myself in such close quarters.

With the arrival of spring, it became somewhat easier to find fruit and vegetables in the fields, although venturing out of the forests entailed ever more risk of discovery. As Germany's situation continued to deteriorate following the beating they received in the famous battle of Kursk, it became increasingly obvious to the local population that the Germans were losing the war. This worked both for and against us. While some people were now more willing to help us, others were now more sharply on the lookout for us so as to win the prizes the Germans offered to any Pole who helped them find and exterminate any Jew, anywhere.

Meanwhile, with so many people in the forest, we sometimes got in each other's way at night when we crawled out of our bunkers. In late May, my family decided that in case the Gestapo or Poles came looking to kill us, it would be best to divide the family. My mother, little sister Rosa—now nine years old—and eleven other people, including Wolf Einspruch, went to live in a bunker under the house of a nice Polish family in a nearby village. The decision to send Rosa instead of another of the siblings was motivated by the fact that she had been suffering with bad colds and bronchitis. The family thought that living in a "house" environment would be better for her health. My mother, too, suffered from circulation and heart problems, and her legs were severely swollen all the time, so we likewise thought it best for her health to leave. Besides that, my mother could not let her youngest child go alone. Again, the altruistic Polish family was well paid, but they also lived under the threat of death.

That June, not long after the move, word somehow got out that this particular Polish family was hiding Jews. No one knows for sure who betrayed them, but neighbors looking for some of that German prize money often talked. They would frequently sniff out something unusual and report it to the police.

The Gestapo and Polish police arrived early one morning and questioned the owner of the house. He denied hiding any Jews anywhere on his property, but they searched anyway, finding straw mats and blankets in the attic that were still warm. The Gestapo officer said, "Look, it's obvious you had Jews here just minutes ago. Show us where they are."

He knew no matter what he said, they were going to kill him, so he didn't say anything, at which point they took him outside and unceremoniously shot him. Then they set fire to the house.

The thirteen Jews were hiding in the bunker under the house. Since smoke rises, they might have been safe; however, cramped into their little ditch, with the flames fully consuming the building and smoke pouring out of every crevice, some of them began to choke, struggling to stifle their coughs as much as possible. Luckily, no one heard them as the house burned to the ground. The Gestapo and police left around noon.

My mother, sister, and the others finally emerged into broad daylight, thinking they had been miraculously saved. Instead, the local peasantry who had been standing around watching the burning spectacle, fell on them with clubs and rakes, and beat them all to death—even my little nine-year-old sister Rosa and that beautiful sixteen-year-old girl Bochner had rescued. The police returned and moved all the bodies to the Jewish cemetery, and even though there was no need to do so, they shot each one to make sure they were all really dead. Only one person managed to escape to tell the tale: Wolf Einspruch. He made it back to the forest that same evening and told us what happened.

It is hard to describe what fury really is, but when I found out that my mother and little sister had been beaten to death and then shot along with all those other people, I went crazy. So did Jozef. We went into a rage beyond description; it was a psychological breaking point. We took off for the town to find the local police commander who had been in charge and avenge our mother's and sister's murders. We didn't even discuss it; we knew without saying a word that we were going to find him and kill him. Neither of us cared what happened to us afterward.

The town was on the opposite side of the river. We knew we had to cross a bridge to get to the other side, and we knew that bridge was guarded by a German soldier. As we headed toward it, I asked: "What are we doing to do when we meet this German guard?"

Without even looking at me, my brother said: "If you ask me one more question, I'll kill you!" And he meant it. He was so crazy out of his mind with anger, and I understood exactly what he felt because it was no different for me. When we got to the bridge, the German soldier said only one word to us: "Dokumente." It was the last thing he ever said. We then proceeded to the home of the police commander, who, as fate would have it, was not home. At that point, we had moved beyond reasonable thought. In our rage, we tore his house apart; we did everything short of burning it down. Afterward, we returned to the forest in a surprising state of calmness.

By November 1942, news of Hitler's Final Solution was available to everyone in the free world. Public reaction "forced" England and

A Family Dies

America to take "immediate" action. But it wasn't until five months later, on April 19, 1943, that British and American officials gathered to discuss the "political refugee problem." They did not want to single out or address the ones who were Hitler's direct and specific targets; they preferred to pretend they were talking about all kinds of people, not just Jews. Hence, they considered the United Nation's suggestion that America try buying refugees— again, Jews and non-Jews—from Hitler. They proposed offering to exchange Nazi and German civilian prisoners for refugees, and they discussed finding a way to send food to those in the concentration camps. They also talked about approaching neutral countries to which they could send refugees in the event they could actually get away from the Germans.

All of these noble concepts were either rejected or tabled for "future" discussion and consideration.

The final report from the British Foreign Secretary notes:

This requires careful handling. It is quite possible that rich Jews will pay large sums of money to escape being murdered by the Huns ... We would be taking great responsibility if we prevented the escape of Jews, even if they should be rich Jews ... After all, they have no doubt paid for their liberation so high that they are poor Jews now and, therefore, have the ordinary rights of human beings.[9]

According to the Shoah Resource Center—the International School for Holocaust Studies—the Bermuda Conference "marked the high point of efforts by officials in both nations to thwart a move for more effective action to rescue European Jewry."[9]

Much has been written about the governments of the world not knowing what was really going on, but it is impossible to pretend the Allies were even slightly unaware of what was happening to Jews. In May that same year, Szmul Zygielbojm, who had escaped after serving on the Judenrat council in the infamous Warsaw ghetto and eventually made his way to London, committed suicide in protest of the Allies' refusal to help the Jews despite all evidence of Germany's genocide policies. Zygielbojm was serving as the Bund Party representative to the Polish National Council in exile when he wrote final letters to a number of friends and newspapers, along with this now-famous missive to the President of Poland:

May 11, 1943

To President W. Raczkiewicz
To the Chairman of the Council of Ministers - W. Sikorski

I take the liberty of addressing to you my last words and through you to the Polish government and people, to the governments and peoples of the Allied states and to the conscience of the world…

The responsibility for the crime of murdering all the Jewish population in Poland falls, in the first instance, on the perpetrators, but indirectly it also burdens the whole of humanity, upon the peoples and governments of the Allied states that, so far, have made no effort towards a concrete action to put a stop to this crime…

A Family Dies

I cannot remain silent. I cannot live while the remnants of the Jewish people in Poland whose representative I am are being exterminated. My comrades in the Warsaw ghetto perished with their weapons in their hands in their last heroic battle. It was not my destiny to die as they did, together with them. But I belong to them and in their mass graves.

By my death I wish to make the strongest possible protest against the passivity with which the world is looking on and permitting the extermination of the Jewish people. I know how little human life is worth today, but as I was unable to do anything during my life, perhaps by my death I shall help to break down the indifference of those who have the possibility now, at the last moment to save those Polish Jews still alive, from certain annihilation.

My life belongs to the Jewish people in Poland and, therefore, I give it to them. I wish that the surviving remnants of the several millions of Polish Jews could live to see, with the Polish population, the liberation that it could know in Poland, in a world of freedom and in the justice of socialism. I believe that such a Poland will arise and that such a world will come.

I bid farewell to everybody and everything that was dear to me and that I have loved.

Szmul Zygielbojm[10]

Nineteen-forty-three was a long summer. Jozef no longer snuck back to our former home to see Ursula. She had taken up with another man, a German soldier, and no longer wanted Jozef to come around. He was distraught, but the rest of us were relieved. We had never been sure if in the heat of the moment he would reveal our location. Their friendship had deep roots and he trusted her, but we did not trust anyone, least of all God. Atheism was the only "religion" that made sense to me.

In early September, my father conceded to letting Nina and me build a new, separate bunker a few hundred yards away from our original one, which now contained eleven men and women, including my father, Jozef, and Wolf. Not long after, on September 13, news reached us that Marshal Pietro Badoglio had capitulated to the Allies in Bari, Italy, and that his country had joined the fight against Germany. We were all overjoyed; the war was definitely turning against the Germans, but we kept our jubilance quiet in our respective bunkers.

A few hours later that same day, a Gestapo unit accompanied by Polish police entered the forest, directing rifle grenades precisely into the large bunker. *Precisely*. From a distance of maybe two hundred yards, they aimed their grenades as if they knew exactly where our bunker was. Obviously, they did.

While my sister and I watched horrified from the safety of our own dugout, the police dragged my father and brother out of the hole. My father's chest was open from the grenade. My brother was badly wounded. One of the Gestapo officers kicked my father. "Tell me who helped you!" My father spat at him.

A Family Dies

The German pulled his revolver and shot him. Then he shot Jozef.

Nina and I stayed hidden just a few hundred yards away while the Germans and Poles shot everyone, buried them in the shallow ditch, and left the forest. The stillness was deafening. We were alone, the sole survivors of our family, the only ones left in our part of the forest. Even Wolf Einspruch hadn't escaped this time. We didn't know where to go. We had no help. Everyone was hostile to us. Our desperate rage, however, was replaced by an enormous sense of loss, fear, and helplessness.

The following night, Nina and I stole into the attic of an abandoned building that had formerly belonged to a Jewish family, but we felt very insecure there; we jumped at every noise, every rat movement. For all we knew, it might have been perfectly safe, but we didn't know the place and felt too threatened to stay there. At the same time we were afraid to stay in the forest, convinced that the Germans would come back for us.

The next night, we snuck out of the attic and into the basement of our rabbi's former house, which we knew very well. That morning, though, we heard disconcerted voices saying they sensed something strange. We jumped out of there and started running back toward the forest, right in broad daylight. It wasn't long before a whole Polish mob was running after us. I was much smaller, lighter, and faster than my sister, who was behind me, trying to catch up. I looked back to say, "Hurry!" as a Polish commander took out his revolver and shot her, right before my eyes.

And so she died. And I kept running.

5

ALONE

1943-1944

I made it to the forest minutes, maybe hours, after Nina was shot. I had no concept of the time involved; I just kept running, pursued by local villagers and the Polish Police, until I disappeared in the trees. Once I was sure they had given up the chase, I collapsed under a tree and cried uncontrollably, unable to think at all. My brain was paralyzed with the pain of what had happened. My entire immediate family was dead. Everyone from my house, everyone who loved me, all slaughtered. All the other people who'd been with us in the forest: dead. Not exterminated by Hitler, not killed in war, not gassed in some hideous death chamber; but rather murdered by our own Polish neighbors, executed in front of me by people who felt no compunction about stripping all the clothes off my father, brother, and the other people in their bunker—including Wolf Einspruch, who had been something of a hero to me—before burying them in that same bunker. The police had "rewarded" them for their malevolence with the victims' clothing.

My mind could not process it all. I was thirteen years old, orphaned, hunted—and all alone. What awaited me now?

This was my darkest hour. I reached my highest point of desperation, not even afraid anymore to cry out loudly. I literally howled like an animal in pain. After that, I never cried out again.

Gradually I regained control over myself and faced my reality lucidly. My first thought was, *now that I'm alone, you will never get me.* I immediately dug a new bunker in the same forest with my bare hands, but a long distance from my previous bunker. Simultaneously, I kept imagining what it would feel like to be shot through the brain. *Would it hurt? How long before I died?* I developed a determination to survive, no matter what, with only one motivation in mind: living long enough to exact revenge. That very morning, the groundwork for my single-focused, widespread, grand-scale daydreaming of vengeance was born.

Immediately following Hitler's invasion of Poland and after myriad machinations between Czechoslovakia, Hungary, and Germany, Jozef Tiso became the *de facto* leader of Slovakia, which at that time had a Jewish population of approximately 80,000. When Hitler imposed his "Final Solution" in 1942, he instructed Tiso, along with the leaders of his other client states, to transport all Slovak Jews to Poland. There's still a good deal of controversy over whether or not the people involved in the process knew they were sending those Jews to certain death, but the good Catholic Monsignor Tiso had uncontested, full knowledge of their destination.

> Historically, an argument has raged over Tiso's position on Jewish policies. Some, such as the historian Milan Durica, believe

Tiso actually helped protect some Jews from deportation, particularly those who benefited the Slovak economy and received exemptions. Others claim Tiso wholeheartedly endorsed and participated in the process, and thus bore full responsibility. Even though Jewish leaders warned Tiso that the deportations might lead to extermination, he did allow them to take place in 1942, and the Slovak government even paid 500 Reichsmarks for each Jew sent to Germany.[11]

When Axis forces occupied Yugoslavia in April 1941, the largest piece of the dismembered country was the Independent State of Croatia, which was ruled by a Nazi puppet government under the direct jurisdiction of the Vatican. Thus Croatia and Slovakia became the only two countries during the Holocaust ruled under direct orders of the Church.[12] Zealot Ante Pavelić, a Croatian bigot and the *de facto* ruler of Croatia, led the Ustaše (Ustashi), a government-sanctioned terrorist group, in a brutal campaign to exterminate Croatia's nearly two million Serbs and other "foreign elements."[13] Non-Catholic Serbs were given the choice to convert or die, while Jews were given no choice. As the Vatican held Jews responsible for killing Jesus, their mass murder was compulsory. In the process of the ensuing forced conversions and religious executions, the Ustashi perpetrated the most hideous savagery of World War II against Orthodox Serbs, Jews, and gypsies. Future UN Secretary General Kurt Waldheim "was a key German officer in the area of the worst massacres ... [who] helped the mass murderer Ante Pavelić ... to such an extent that Pavelić awarded Waldheim one of the highest decorations—a medal with oak-leaf clusters."[14]

Vjekoslav Luburić, the commander-in-chief of all the Croatian concentration camps, once proudly announced, "We have slaughtered here at Jasenovac more people than the Ottoman Empire was able to do during its occupation in Europe."[15]

The German killing machine was so thorough that no Jew escaped its clutches.

When the Germans occupied Guernsey, a tiny English channel island, a Rolls-Royce driving English policeman delivered the sole Jewish family residing there to the local German commander. The entire family was promptly dispatched to Auschwitz.

About 20,000 Jews lived on the Greek Island of Rhodes. Following the German occupation, all were rounded up and shipped out for transportation to Auschwitz. When the captain of the ship radioed to the German Admiralty in Berlin as to the final destination of his cargo and passengers, he was told they were consigned to the Final Solution. That radio message was intercepted by Ultra, a British counterspy organization working out of Bletchly, England. The man who intercepted the message—a German Jewish refugee—immediately understood the meaning of the term Final Solution and reported its sinister significance to his superiors. They advised him not to mention it to anyone again.

Though I didn't learn about many of these atrocities until much later, I had witnessed enough by that time in my rather insulated world to equal my future knowledge of what the Holocaust had done to the Jews of Europe. For all the innocent mothers, fathers, children, grandchildren—all the horribly terrorized, mutilated, ravaged, murdered souls—I vowed to seek revenge. But first, I had to survive in a place where no one else I knew had.

I lived alone in the forest with wild animals as my only companions, focused on daily survival. I was wretched, desperately alone, and well aware I'd been branded an outlaw to be hunted down and shot where found. That winter, I suffered the worst periods of cold and hunger. Often I could not sneak onto farms in search of food, or find any food at all. Most days I subsisted on tree bark, moss, roots, and needles. My only saving grace was that winter days were short and few people ventured into the forest.

The nights belonged to me. When I was lucky, I raided Polish farms in the darkness and stole what I could to eat. Snow served as water. Having lost my stolen knife, I stole an axe from a farmer, though I remembered how useless it had been for my Uncle Joseph when he used one to defend himself against the Polish police. They had easily dodged his clumsy swings and smashed his head with their rifle butts. Nevertheless, the axe provided me some comfort as I moved from place to place, in constant terror of being caught and disposed of like the savage I was rapidly becoming. The one thing done to my family and me that I could not forgive or forget was that of being reduced to the status of a wild animal.

One particular night, I decided to hide in a fairly spacious Christian mausoleum. I sat there until dawn, feeling relatively secure in the knowledge that no one would enter the place unless to commemorate some relative, and that would only be during the day. A few hours after daybreak, a young boy named Julek—who I knew both as a former neighbor and classmate—came wandering through the cemetery to visit his family's grave. He instantly recognized me and appeared shocked to find me there. I, in turn, was afraid he would reveal my presence to his family and they would tell the police. My first instinct was to strangle him in self-defense, but because we knew each other so well, I simply begged him not to reveal my whereabouts to anyone. He assured me he would not, and I refrained from harming him. Nevertheless, I was uneasy after he departed.

As soon as I knew he was gone, I left the mausoleum and climbed one of the big oak trees that stood in the cemetery a short distance away. Being small and agile, I was able to climb well out of sight in the tree's upper branches. No less than two hours later, Polish police dressed in blue and Gestapo officers dressed in green entered the graveyard and began searching the mausoleum and cemetery grounds. Fortunately, they did not bring any dogs.

Even today, it is inconceivable to me how this boy with whom I had studied in the same classroom and happily played soccer could have betrayed me, having full knowledge of the lethal consequences that would result. My only regret was having trusted him—and not having choked him when I had the chance.

By spring, the fields were abundant with fruit and vegetables. I would forage through them at night and steal turnips, potatoes, or whatever edible I could find. I was acutely aware that venturing out of the forest this way was risky. If anyone heard or saw me, my life would be over. I always had to stop and listen every few steps, then rearrange the path if I was going through wheat fields or the like so as not to leave any traces on the ground.

One night I sensed someone stalking me. I couldn't pinpoint who or where; I simply felt it. As I took slower, more cautious steps, a boy suddenly appeared out of nowhere and without a word jumped on me and pinned me to the ground. The fact that he acted so silently told me he must not be an enemy; a German or Pole would have blocked me with shouts and insults.

"Who are you?" he demanded in a whisper.

What could I say? "I'm a Jew."

"Speak Yiddish if you really are Jewish."

So I repeated that I was Jewish in Yiddish. At that point he released me and I stood up. We looked at each other.

"Do you know who I am?" he asked.

At that moment, I recognized him as Isaak Stern from my own town. He was a few years older than I was, a fine young man Nina had admired from a relatively wealthy family of store owners. At the start of the war he'd been a student at the gymnasium, a remarkable accomplishment for a Jew. Only exceptional students in rare cases broke the *numerus clausus* (closed number) barrier. To me, Isaak represented the best of our Pilzno youth, a model of extreme intellect and gentility.

He recognized me as well and we embraced. I felt profound joy in encountering Isaak; I felt as if I had found a brother who extinguished the terrible longing I had for human contact. We remained there talking for a few minutes before I asked if I could go with him, to fight it out together. He explained kindly but firmly that our chances for survival were much better if we were each alone. He wasn't going to ask where I was going, and he wouldn't tell me where he was going; it would be safer that way, in case one of us was captured. He spoke to me with heartfelt kindness and tenderness about the need for separation. I begged him to take me with him, but even in the face of my tears, he convinced me to stay. In reality, I perfectly understood his position. My brief time with him was both the happiest and most heart-wrenching time during my survival. We parted in the dark of night, each going our own way in silence. I never saw Isaak Stern alive again.

It was a late spring or early summer evening in 1944 when I hid myself and waited in the garden of my old house for Mrs. Hurkova to come out alone. Her family was so imbued with Nazism it would have been suicidal for me to make contact with their knowledge.

I had given a lot of thought to approaching our former friend. I knew that if Mrs. Hurkova had returned the equivalent of about fifty dollars to my father when he asked for it, she might have helped his survival in strange, indescribable ways. I was certain she was aware that I knew she had refused. She knew about the killings of my entire family; the whole town knew. They also all knew I was still alive.

When Mrs. Hurkova discovered me in our garden that evening, I sensed a strong feeling of guilt in her, and she shed some heavy tears about my father. I didn't know if they were honest tears or not, because I also sensed another emotion in her: fear. By that time, the Soviet Army was only a couple hundred miles away, and Mrs. Hurkova was worried about what would happen to her and her family when the Soviets moved into our Polish town and found a German family living in the home of slaughtered Jews. The war was going very badly for the Germans; she was both afraid of staying and reluctant to run back to Germany, knowing the Soviets would catch up with her.

With all this in mind, I asked her to let me stay in the attic of a storage shed without anyone in her family's knowing. In exchange, I assured her I would be her protector when the Soviets arrived, telling them how much she had helped me. She reluctantly agreed and provided me with water and just enough food to keep me from starving.

I knew better than to truly trust anyone, so the first thing I did was create an escape route just in case Mrs. Hurkova betrayed me and I got surrounded. At that point all I had was my little penknife, but I was very skinny, so I only needed a small opening to slip through. I waited until night, then used a stone to hammer on the knife to cut out my escape hole. Every time I hit that stone on the penknife, Mrs. Hurkova's family came running out to investigate. As superstition was quite real and present among the locals, they proclaimed: "It's a ghost of the Jews." As soon as they went back in the house, I started cutting again. I finally broke through the shed's ceiling, achieving a slender, easily overlooked hole that allowed me to lower myself down from the attic. In those days I could climb like a cat anywhere. After I was finished, the penknife broke in half.

I remained sufficiently hidden until one day that summer when I watched through my peephole as a convoy of German trucks passed right outside my hiding place. Suddenly, a squadron of American planes appeared out of nowhere. I don't know where they were headed—they were on course to bomb Auschwitz if they had wanted to but, of course, no one ever did—but they must have spotted the Germans on the road because they swiftly attacked the convoy with bombs and machine-gun fire. I was in disbelief and beyond scared that after all I had endured, I could be killed by one of these bombs falling right next to my shed.

When the German convoy stopped on the road, I descended through my escape hole into the shed below. Just as I landed in a crouch, one of the German soldiers trying to hide from the machine guns ran into the shed, and I found myself face to face with a German soldier only a few feet away. I knew I looked like a monster. I hadn't had a haircut for years. My clothes had disintegrated into rags and I had no shoes, only more rags around my feet. I was horrified by my appearance and terrified of him at the same time, but I quickly realized he was even more frightened of me.

The attack outside lasted only a few minutes. We remained still, staring at each other. I kept my hand under my rags as if I was pointing a gun at him. He had to have been a fool to think I had a weapon, but he was obviously too frightened to think rationally. He tried to back out the door slowly without turning around, but no sooner had he stepped outside when his superior officer appeared and began cursing him. "You are the worst! I'm going to court martial you and shoot you on the spot for deserting your machine gun!"

"But look who's inside here," the soldier tried to say.

"One more word out of you and I'll have you shot right now! Just shut up and get on the truck."

The soldier obeyed and as it started to drive off, he turned toward me one more time as if to say: *Boy, are you lucky*. He couldn't tell anyone I was in there, so they drove off.

And I survived another day.

6

GROWN-UP CHILD

August 1944

Germany was losing the war, and the Soviets were progressing steadily westward. In late August 1944, a motorcycle bearing a red star drove very slowly from the east along the road outside my shed. I was dazed and giddy; in a few minutes, I imagined I would be free. Instead, the motorcycle turned around right in front of my hiding place and headed back east. About ten minutes later, another motorcycle appeared, this time coming from the west and bearing a German swastika. It was followed by a panzer unit of tanks and other armored vehicles. The convoy stopped in the middle of the road. A senior German officer wearing goggles—looking exactly like the Nazi officers later depicted in every Hollywood movie—stood up in his open vehicle, declared the entire area a military zone, and ordered his junior officer to "expel all these Polish swine." They were given two hours, but the entire civilian population, including the Hurkovas, was gone within one.

In order to survive at this point, I either had to pretend I was a Pole and leave with the others or stay in the military zone among the Germans. It was not a hard decision; I knew my former neighbors would immediately recognize me and either kill me themselves or turn me over to the Germans to be shot. I chose to stay in the attic, amongst the German Army, with the Polish torturers finally off my back.

German soldiers started building a bunker right below me. I could listen to their discussions and smell their food, which made clear the biggest hole in my plan. Now that Mrs. Hurkova was gone, where was I going to get food? From the Germans' conversation, I knew that the Soviets had stopped and set up their own military zone about two miles away, just across the Wisloka river. They were so close, in fact, that I could hear them playing their accordions and singing their songs at night. I briefly entertained the idea of trying to run through the German lines to the Soviet camp where I might beg for food, but I knew the plan was futile. I would be shot at from both sides with no chance of making it. The question therefore became how to get food where I was, in the middle of the enemy's encampment.

I was still a child, but I made an important observation right away. The bunker below me was manned by two German soldiers who rotated in two-hour shifts. After one shift ended, the man on guard would leave and call the other soldier to relieve him. This usually left an interval of about five minutes when the bunker was unattended. I could drop down from my attic, dash out the door, steal some of their food, and be back in the safety of my attic before the replacement guard arrived.

One day I made a terrible mistake. I not only stole bread, but I also stole some sausage. The next day, I could plainly hear one guard say to the other, "Hans, I have to talk to you. I noticed lately that you are stealing my food. I don't mind you stealing my bread, but I especially resent your stealing the sausage that my mother just sent to me from Berlin. Please don't steal that."

I never again stole sausage; I confined my pilfering to bread, sardines, and similar foods. I also stole the soldiers' newspapers, which were normally no more than two days old. Being fluent in German, I could read what the allies were doing in France and what was happening in Italy, but I never knew what was happening one hundred yards away from me beyond what the guards might say to each other. They did not seem to be in any hurry for the eventual battle to begin. Being in a location vulnerable to shelling from either side, neither was I.

I learned to utilize those five-minute guard-changing intervals to my best advantage, being careful to raid the bunker erratically so the two soldiers would not notice a pattern. I could not leave the area, of course, but I could dash out while the trench was empty to find water and take care of my personal needs, then hide until the next five-minute interval, when I would slip back to the safety of my attic hideaway. It was a risky arrangement, but it worked.

Life went on this way, hour after hour, day after day, week after week, month after month. I had no one to talk to; there was nowhere I could go. I couldn't even return to the forest because German soldiers were everywhere. Overall, I felt safer than when I had to fear the local population, but I was lonely, hungry, and bored, and I was always aware of the chance I'd be discovered.

Occasionally, both armies exchanged some fire but none of any great consequence. It seemed obvious that the fighting was paused while both sides prepared for new battles. I spent my days reading stolen newspapers and my nights listening to the Soviets' music. It was a chilly fall and a cold winter; and although I had to be careful not to walk around during the day so that the Germans below would not hear, at least I was better off inside the shed than

I had been the previous winter, trapped in a freezing hole in the ground with the police and citizenry actively searching for me.

There was quite a bit of hay in the attic, and I hid within it at night, covering myself completely. I had to be careful not to sneeze or cough; I even felt I had to control my sleep as I was afraid of producing unconscious sounds and being discovered. I had to be totally still and silent. Overall though, unless I made a stupid mistake, no one would realize I existed.

On January 15, 1945, I watched some of the Germans roll up a huge reel of cables, load it onto a truck, then drive away. They had never done that before, which gave me the impression that something was happening. The very next morning, just as the bells rang six o'clock in the Catholic church a few miles away, the Soviets let loose with an intense bombardment on the German encampment. The barrage lasted two hours as German soldiers and officers were destroyed right in front of me. As it came to an end, I overheard the two soldiers I had come to know in the bunker below.

"Hans, let's run!"

"Just give me a chance to put my boots on—"

"There's no time for that!"

And thus I watched this highly organized, empire-like army that had frightened me so terribly when it swept into Poland in 1939 now flee like rats without time to put on their shoes. I saw the last deserting soldier run past my shed barefoot. It was a great moment of triumph for me.

The Soviet artillery stopped around eight o'clock. Total quiet prevailed, except for the shrieks of the wounded soldiers left behind by their fleeing comrades. Otherwise, the Germans were gone. The townspeople had been gone for months; there was no sign of the Soviets arriving. I was truly the only person in town who was alive.

I slipped down from the attic and stepped out of the shed into the broad daylight. German soldiers and officers lay all around me, dead or too wounded to move. I could not resist the temptation. I went from one officer to another and grabbed each by the shirtfront. "Look at me!" I screamed. "Do you know who I am? I'm a Jew! See, it is not *Judenrein*! You did not purify! I am Jewish!"

Many of them begged for water. I knew how it felt to be horribly thirsty. I'd been hungry and thirsty for over three years. But I also vividly remembered those truckloads of Soviet prisoners, and how the smug young German guards had bayoneted their palms when they reached out to catch a few drops of rainwater. So I answered each one with, "No water."

The day went by. There were still no other Poles, Germans, or Jews to be seen. No Soviets either. The sun sets early in January, and as darkness set in, I heard soldiers marching in the distance. I could tell by the sound of their cadence that they were not Germans; their tread was completely unlike that of German units. Soon, I saw a unit of soldiers moving in my direction from the east. As they got closer, I suddenly dashed out in front of them, frantically hoping they were Soviets. Indeed they were—and so were their automatic pistols, which they immediately surrounded me with.

Their leader tried to ask me some questions, but I didn't speak Russian, so I spoke to him in Polish, which he did not understand.

Finally he tried a German dialect that I immediately recognized as Yiddish.

"In which direction did the last Germans leave?" He asked.

When I answered him in Yiddish, he threw his arms around me and hugged me. He had tears in his eyes. "For the last couple hundred kilometers, I haven't encountered a single Jew," he said. "Don't worry, the Germans are not coming back here. You'll see our tanks here in a couple of hours."

And so it was. I, the only one of my family—and from what I could tell, my entire community—had survived the war. My liberators were marching in. I was "free."

Two women doctors were part of the first group that followed the tanks in that evening. They spotted me and were appalled by my appearance. I was filthy from head to toe, my hair long and matted and grimy, my feet barely shod in newspaper-stuffed shoes that a German had left behind. I'd turned fifteen less than two months earlier, but I was so short and malnourished that I still looked like a little boy.

The lady doctors immediately bathed me, gave me new clothing, and made up a clean bed with fresh linen. After hiding in the attic of my own house for weeks, I was able to sleep in a normal bed—my own bed—for the first time in years, awash in conflicting emotions of relief and gratitude, loss and grief. When I woke up, the doctors brought in their superiors, asking me to describe my experiences and how I had survived. They were aghast at what I'd lived through, at what had been perpetrated on a child. At that point, none of us yet knew about the horrors done to countless, less fortunate children in the death camps. The only thing I knew at that moment was what the Germans had done to me personally. They had robbed me of my childhood, my family, my friends, my neighbors. Everybody.

With that knowledge alone, I remained staunch in my primary goal: Revenge.

The townspeople returned to their homes the next day on January 17, 1945, along with the few other Jewish survivors. Out of the initial 1,342 souls in our community, only sixteen remained. Many of my neighbors greeted me like a long-lost son, claiming they had tried to help us survive but feared being shot for doing so. Some were outright hostile: "Too bad they didn't get you too," was a common greeting. Most were terribly afraid of returning Jews, who would naturally wish to reclaim the homes and businesses that were seized and occupied since the day we had been rounded up into the ghetto.

In the last stages of the war, these hostile Poles had formed an underground militia known as A.K. (Armia Krajova, or Home Army) for the sole purpose of exterminating any remaining Jews who had managed to survive Hitler's Final Solution. The A.K. frequently set up roadblocks to remove any Jew from passing vehicles and simply shot him on the spot. They found Isaak Stern; his body was discovered in one of the fields outside of town, riddled with fresh bullet holes. Fortunately, the KGB garrison set up its headquarters in the building next to my house. I stayed close to home that first day or two, and therefore felt well protected from the town's hostile population.

Most of the Soviets who came in after the bombardment did not stay. I watched as one unit led a group of barefooted German POWs eastward through the snow. Suddenly, the Germans broke out of their column en masse and tried to commit suicide by throwing themselves under a convoy of Soviet trucks moving in the opposite direction. A cordon of Soviet troops just as swiftly formed a human chain to stop them. I enjoyed watching that spectacle, the dismal fate of these formerly arrogant, brutal men. What a difference four years had made for those of us lucky enough to bear witness. It gave me my first taste of revenge—but it wasn't enough.

That same day, I arranged with my new KGB friends to have a party, celebrating with a public hanging of Polish collaborators and Jew killers in the town square. But Hershel Bochner, the man who had snuck my sister Nina into the labor camp for three months and whose family my father had then helped save, suddenly appeared and stopped me cold. "You're too young to realize the effect of this on the rest of the survivors," he said. Consequently, the plan was discarded. Bochner may have been right, but to this day, I still wonder. At that time, all I felt was my overpowering desire for retribution and my frustration at having it ripped away from me.

The one person I did not want to take revenge against was Mrs. Hurkova. When she and her family returned to town that same day, I welcomed them to share our former home. The furnishings were exactly as if we had never left. The house had stood empty since the occupation as the German garrison had stayed in their street bunkers or in their tanks and trucks. The Hurkovas accepted my hospitality, but the entire family gave me the silent treatment with barely a phrase exchanged between us, except for Ursula, who cried bitterly over Jozef's death. Like the Poles, they resented me for surviving and repossessing my family's home and belongings, although Mrs. Hurkova claimed to be happy to find me still alive.

The very next day, Polish Security officers (the new Polish KGB) arrived to question Mrs. Hurkova regarding her German background. I did everything in my power to protect her, but to no avail. The security officer arrested her and her entire family as enemies of the state. He showed no sympathy for my pleadings that Mrs. Hurkova had saved not only my life, but probably those of countless other Jews. When I persisted, he turned on me, pulled out his revolver, and pressed it hard against my heart. "Which side are you on, little Jew boy, theirs or ours?" In that instant, I saw the old face of Polish anti-Semitism clearly visible, almost as if he wanted to punish Mrs. Hurkova just for helping Jews. She and I both wept as she was led away, never to be seen again. I was bereft over the loss of my protector but could not help but wonder: *Had she ever really cried for my father and mother—her supposed friends—or were her tears for her fate alone?* Regardless, with her son Walter dead at the hands of the French underground, my life's personal devastation that had begun less than half a decade earlier was now complete: everyone who had ever occupied our house was dead.

Except me.

7

HAVING CHOICES, MAKING CHOICES

January 1945

Within two or three days of the liberation, all the surviving Jews of our community decided to identify the burial sites of our loved ones, as well as those not related to us, and relocate them into a mass grave in the local Jewish cemetery. We hired several Poles to do the excavations and transport the victims on horse-drawn carriages. The whole process was completed in one day. I could not locate the exact site of my mother and sister Rosa in that cemetery, so their bodies remained wherever the Poles buried them after senselessly shooting them. We did exhume my father, Nina, Jozef, Wolf, and the rest of the people who had been killed in the forest. I still clearly remember seeing the bodies in my father's bunker. In the long, horrendous series of life-changing moments I'd lived through, that was one of many that would stay with me forever.

We decided to put up a massive monument inscribed with the names and ages of the victims, including my mother and Rosa. It was constructed some six months after the exhumation and reburying. The actual unveiling of the monument, when they removed the wooden planks from the cement, came about a year later. By that time I had left Pilzno, so I was absent from the ceremony. The monument still stands today, the only commemorative stone in that once ancient Jewish cemetery.

Life returned to as much a state of "normalcy" as it could in our now tiny Jewish community. Monek Schus, one of my Jewish neighbors who had survived the war in the Soviet Union, arrived back in town on a motorcycle a day or so after the Hurkovas were taken away. He came from a large religious family with a substantial estate. We were only three years apart in age and had played soccer before the war. We embraced like brothers. Naturally, he wanted to know what had happened to his family. I had to inform him they were all gassed at Belzec.

We took to exploring the surrounding little towns on his motorcycle to see who else had survived. In those days the Soviet Army drove mostly American Ford trucks under the so-called "Lend Lease" program. The trouble was that most of the Soviet soldiers were perpetually drunk on vodka and had never heard of speed limits. They "flew" those vehicles as if they were airplanes. A few days after Monek's return, we were passing on the main street of Tarnów when a convoy of Soviet trucks came flying at us from the opposite direction. They hit the motorcycle full force, sending it—and us—into the air like a balloon. I landed in a water-filled ditch totally unharmed. Monek died instantly. As I mourned yet another friend I was forced to add to my losses, I gave him a Jewish burial in Tarnów and erected a monument for him.

The local commander of the Soviet KGB unit, at that time known as NKVD, was an interesting character named David Davidovich.

Russians use patronymics, so if your father's name was David, you were David Davidovich. The commander was bemedaled, like so many of them were, carrying honors for the defense of Stalingrad and Leningrad. Commander Davidovich and I became quite friendly, and he repeatedly told me that after the war was over, he would take me back to Leningrad with him and make me into a good communist. "Then you will be able to do all the great things I did," he said. He didn't realize I had other agendas, but he was my personal protector and an interesting character to be around, and I learned a fair amount of Russian listening to the discussions between him and his junior officers.

One day, about two weeks after the liberation, a Polish peasant lady came into the KGB headquarters and approached me with purpose. "I have to talk to you," she said. "I have a neighbor. She has a child. That child is Jewish. We knew it through the war but didn't want to repeat it to anyone for fear of us all getting shot. The mother who left the child did so to save its life. But we feel it's not right that this family should now keep this child as their own."

I agreed and conceded to hitchhike to the nearest Jewish agency, an already functioning Zionist organization, where I spoke with a lawyer named Cohen. I told him he had to go rescue the little girl.

Cohen looked at me and shook his head. "You must be crazy. If I send anybody out to that village, the Poles will kill him. I'm not going to have someone killed to rescue a child."

I became very upset by this. What if someone could have rescued my little sister? There were so few of us left. I could not bear to do nothing. I talked to Davidovich about it, but he too shook his head. "Yes, I'm Jewish," he said, as he had many times before, "but I'm not here by Jewish causes. I'm a communist, and

I'm here to keep communist order." But I was so visibly upset and sad that after a few minutes, he relented. "I'll tell you what. I see it's important to you. Let me introduce you to one of my sergeants. He might be able to help you."

The sergeant Davidovich brought in was of Mongolian background. The first thing he said to me was, "I hate Poles." I offered to pay him in vodka if he would help me rescue the girl.

"Do you know how to ride a bicycle?" he asked.

"Yes."

"Good. Wait here."

He immediately returned with two bicycles. "Let's go to that village."

We rode out to the house. The lady who let us in denied having any Jewish child, so the sergeant pulled out his automatic weapon and shot a few rounds. Suddenly, the child materialized. She was young and frightened, but she was quite willing to come with us.

We took a little horse carriage from the family, loaded our bicycles and the girl on it, and drove off toward the Jewish agency about twenty miles away. Fifteen minutes later, a Polish militia of about ten came after us on bicycles. The Russian, who was half drunk, stood up in the carriage and said, "Just look what I do." He let the A.K. peddle toward us until they got very close, at which point he raised his automatic and called them all kinds of derogatory names for being Polish. "You either go away or I will destroy you all!" As one frightened entity, they turned back. It was a glorious sight.

We continued on and I brought the child to Cohen at the Zionist organization. When he heard our story, he said, "It's got to be crazy what you did. But with boys like you, I'm sure we'll have our state soon." I left the girl with Cohen, certain she would go on to Palestine—which, I found out some forty years later, she did.

I still had to find my own food and money, but I was used to that. Having grown up with a very successful merchant father, I knew how to sell and fortunately now had something unusual to offer: Russian military goods that I could sell to the Poles. On one occasion, I was hitchhiking by truck to Kraków to sell some Russian goods at market when my fellow passengers decided I must be Jewish and should therefore be thrown out of the moving vehicle and killed. I managed to avoid that fate through providence or fast talking, but when we arrived in Kraków and I descended from the truck, I noticed a policeman and immediately related my experience to him. He strolled up to the truck and addressed my tormentors. "So, you were going to kill the little Jew boy. Well, why haven't you done it?"

It's fair to say about ten percent of Jewish survivors in Poland were murdered by the A.K. After I completed my business (and from then on), I only hitchhiked on Soviet military vehicles.

At one point, Commander Davidovich asked what he could do for me, and I was ready with an answer: "Let me accompany your army. I want to see the conquest of Berlin."

"That I can arrange easily," he said. And he did.

He attached me to an army unit where I was "adopted" by the senior officer. By now, I had gained a better grasp of the Russian language and could translate between Russian, Polish, and German. I soon became a "pet" of the unit. Whenever we arrived at a town, the Soviets normally took over the nicest building for their headquarters, and I slept in the same quarters. I not only witnessed their discussions, but they occasionally asked for my help in interrogating German officers, which felt heavenly.

Once we got underway, our advance into Germany was rapid. We were on the move and in a new location daily while the German military disintegrated. I was simply amazed at the sheer number of tanks rumbling through the German countryside. Of course, as I mentioned before, most of the Soviet soldiers driving them were utterly intoxicated.

One day on our march to Berlin, we came into a little town called Sagan. Upon interrogating some of the local people, the Soviets learned that the town had contained a prisoner-of-war camp, Luft Stalag III, which had housed shot-down American, British, Australian, and Canadian pilots during the war. At one point, the prisoners had staged a daring widespread escape. Most were eventually recaptured, and fifty of them were taken to a field and shot by order of their captors.[16]

As word of this spread from one Russian to the next, they became uncontrollably furious and embarked on a rampage of rape and plunder. I remembered how crazy and enraged Jozef and I had felt when we heard about our mother and little sister. These soldiers, however, had weapons and the strength of numbers. They went berserk and practically tore that town apart. I must admit, it felt rather satisfying.

At one point, an old German man around seventy years old demanded to speak to the Soviet commander. He couldn't speak Russian but I was there, so the soldiers took me along to translate. The German berated the Soviet commander of the town: "What kind of people are you? What kind of uncivilized conduct are you allowing here? You are on a rampage! You are behaving like barbarians. What kind of morality and culture can explain such conduct?"

As I translated that, the Soviet officer himself became enraged. "How dare you lecture us about morality and culture!" he screamed. "Don't you know what your people did to us?" Furious beyond control, he whipped out his pistol and shot the old German right in front of me.

Was it sweet revenge? I thought about my grandfather, also in his seventies, driven to suicide after humiliation at the hands of the "cultured" Germans and felt no remorse. Many years later, when I saw the movie *The Great Escape* and realized its connection to the aforementioned events, I remembered the incident and realized I still felt no twinge of conscience over the old German's death.

Traveling with the Soviet army unit, in fact, did much to help my need for what modern society calls closure and what I admit to as revenge. As we advanced further toward Berlin, a soldier reported that a messenger from General Vlasov's army had come into camp. Vlasov's army was composed entirely of former Soviet prisoners of war who had volunteered to fight under German tutelage. There were actually hundreds of thousands of them. They now requested permission to surrender rather than fight against their own brothers.

"Tell the soldier," the commander said, "to return to his unit with this message: 'All are welcome to return and will be given the opportunity to rehabilitate themselves for their past actions.'"

Upon hearing this, the messenger promptly ran off to give the good news to his comrades and superiors. The Soviet senior officer then called for a bottle of vodka and, after a few gulps, issued an order: "As soon as those Vlasovite traitors start approaching Soviet lines, open an artillery barrage and wipe them out. Make sure none survive."

We went on to Berlin, about forty to fifty miles further west. Though I was not a combatant, I was privileged to witness the conquest of Berlin itself. I watched as the Soviet's twenty armies, 6,300 tanks, and 8,500 aircraft crushed the city. I had no regrets about the local population's suffering, no feelings of sympathy for the German bodies hung on every tree and lamppost by Soviet fanatics. I regarded it as justice done. The joy of seeing the red flag planted on the Reichstag, which I witnessed with my own eyes, undid much of the suffering I had gone through.

It was a great day.

8

A BRIEF RESPITE

June 1945

I stayed in Berlin with my adopted Russian unit through Hitler's death and the complete capture of the city. By June 1945, I was ready to return to Pilzno.

It took eight days of hitchhiking on Russian military vehicles for me to get home. By the time I got back, the local KGB station was closed and David Davidovich was nowhere to be found. I went to my house, but feeling the wrath of the Polish A.K., I left the same day. I was afraid to remain there even one night, and I sold my house and everything in it for a pittance. One of my neighbors offered me the one hundred and fifty American dollars hidden under his bed, and since the house was no use to me and I knew the money would help somewhere, I took it. I had only a small valise of things and the clothes I was wearing.

One of the other Pilzno survivors, a former rabbinical student named Roman Taub, decided to stay and become an ardent communist.

"Why?" I asked incredulously.

"I want to become Chief Prosecutor in Warsaw," he replied coldly, "so that any Pole who appears before my court, no matter why, will be sentenced to hang."

He achieved his dream, and eventually died in a Warsaw prison for those crimes.

The rest of my fellow survivors had already scattered in different directions. Polish anti-Semitism was as rampant as ever, if not worse. As most of the 250,000 Jews returned from Russia and central Asia, they continued across the border into Germany, where they were placed in so-called "displaced persons" camps run by the United Nations Relief and Works Agency (UNRWA). UNRWA helped thousands of people regain their health after the near-starvation existence in concentration camps, and they aided tens of thousands in relocating to America, Australia, Canada, and later, Israel. People in UNRWA camps remained refugees for the duration of their processing, which took anywhere from a few weeks to several months to a couple of years.

Ironically, as of 1948, UNRWA switched to taking care of Palestinian refugees—not merely to help them regain their health, find work, and become contributing members of society, but to support them from cradle to grave. Today UNRWA, renamed the United Nations Relief and Works Agency for Palestine Refugees in the Near East, is a relief and human development agency, providing education, healthcare, social services, and emergency aid to over 4.6 million refugees living in the Gaza Strip, the West Bank, Jordan, Lebanon, and the Syrian Arab Republic. As the largest UN operation in the Middle East with over 29,000 staff—almost all of them refugees themselves—UNRWA workers contribute directly as teachers, doctors, nurses, or social workers to benefit their communities.[17]

So while Holocaust refugees were helped on their way back to society by UNRWA, Palestinian "refugees" are born, raised, and die under the UNRWA umbrella of care, which is almost entirely funded by the United States. With free food, clothing, shelter, and education for their entire lives, they have nothing to do except sit in cafés and plan bombings; thus, the Palestinian people have remained "refugees" for generations, going so far as to create, with the help of UNRWA, a recognized refugee society—the ultimate oxymoron.

But the Palestinians were not the only people the world reached out to help. While scores of countries had turned their backs on the plight of millions of innocent Jews being murdered, many of them opened their arms to the Nazis who committed the butchery. Beginning with Catholic Bishop Alois Hudal, rector of the Austrian and German Pontificio Istituto Teutonico di Santa Maria dell'Anima seminary in Rome and "Spiritual Director of the German People resident in Italy," and continuing with a group of Croatian priests headed up by Father Krunoslav Draganović, also based in Rome, the Catholic Church did everything it could to help former Nazis escape the consequences of their actions. As Hudal wrote in his memoirs:

> I thank God that He [allowed me] to visit and comfort many victims in their prisons and concentration camps and to help them escape with false identity papers.[18]

> The Allies' War against Germany was not a crusade, but the rivalry of economic complexes for whose victory they had been fighting. This so-called business ... used catchwords like democracy, race, religious liberty and Christianity as a bait for the masses. All these experiences were the reason why I felt duty bound after 1945 to devote my whole charitable work mainly to

former National Socialists and Fascists, especially to so-called 'war criminals'.[19]

The good priests provided such misunderstood men as Josef Mengele, Ante Pavelic, and Adolph Eichmann—among hundreds of others—with money, falsified documents, and Vatican-sanctioned papers that allowed them to obtain displaced-person passports from the International Red Cross, followed by visas. The church's stamp of approval was all that was necessary for these "German-speaking civil internees" to gain legitimate passports and secret "back-door" passage via Scandinavia, Switzerland, and Belgium to Argentina, where the infamous Juan Perón greeted them with rescue teams, citizenship, and employment.

Such was the fate of some of the worst mass-murderers in history—a far cry from the aid and assistance offered to their millions upon millions of innocent victims.

I left Pilzno and its rising anti-Semitism behind and hitchhiked to Beuthen, a German town just across the border, now annexed to Poland and called Bytom. A beautiful city full of equally beautiful parks, Bytom was just a five-minute tram ride away from Gliwice, where Hitler had staged his *causus bellum* at the local radio station. A couple hundred thousand Germans must have lived in Bytom before the war, but the Poles had expelled them all back to Germany. When I got there the town was practically empty. Anyone of Polish nationality could come in and take an apartment of their choice, so I ensconced myself in a nice German apartment. It was not long, however, before the town rapidly filled with Poles from Eastern Poland, which had been taken over by the Soviet Union. Total chaos reigned; no two people knew each other. After awhile, a small group of Jewish-Russian expatriates—including me—formed a community of survivors. We would get together and discuss what to do next and where to go; we all knew we could not stay in Poland. The influx of Poles hated us as much here as they had in our former *shtetls*.

Though I stayed in Bytom for only a short time, it was longer than I had lived in the shed over the German bunker. The one hundred and fifty dollars I brought with me kept me fed and allowed me to make short journeys around the area. I was still alone, but like the rest of the survivors, I did my best to bury the horrors of the war and get on with my life, grateful to be one of the handful left alive. I spent most of my days walking around the city, enjoying the peaceful beauty of the parks.

Early in spring 1946, I heard a rumor that some rabbi was looking for Jewish orphans who had survived the war to transport them to England. I quickly discovered it was more than just hearsay, so I took the next train to Warsaw to look up Rabbi Solomon Schonfeld. The Chief Chaplain to the British Army, he was a wonderful man, tall and very good looking as a military person. He spoke fluent German because he had gotten his rabbinate from a famous yeshiva in Königsberg, which used to be the heart of Prussia—now Kaliningrad—so we communicated easily.[20] As soon as I found him I said, "I hear you are looking for Jewish orphans."

He shook his head sadly. "You are too late. I had one hundred visas and I used them all up. I can't take you." Then he said, "What are you going to do now?"

I was very quick on my feet. "Rabbi, don't worry," I said. "I'll just convert to Catholicism and I'll be okay here."

He grabbed my arm. "You'll do nothing of the sort! Come with me to the British embassy."

At that time, all the foreign embassies were located in Hotel Polonia. It was the one building in that area of Warsaw that had not been destroyed in the war, probably because it had been the German army headquarters until the bitter end. Ironically, Hotel Polonia was located on Jerusalem Avenue, which revealed its history: the area had been full of Jews at one time.

We went right up to see the British ambassador. I didn't understand much of what was said, just a few words in English from my parents having lived in the US, but I understood clearly when he pulled a piece of paper out of a drawer, stamped it twice, and held it out to me.

"Now we have a visa for you," said the rabbi. "You'll be number 101."

It was my first airplane ride on which the rabbi flew us from Gdynia to board a Swedish boat, the SS Ragner. I had never been out of the Poland/Germany area before, and this was also my first sea voyage. We went to England by passing through the so-called Kiel, which is a German canal linking the Baltic Sea to the North Sea. It was the last time I saw German officials.

Our first stop after crossing the canal was Trelleborg, a small town in Sweden. The young children in town had found out about all the orphans coming in on the ship, so they came down to the docks to greet us. They were very friendly, greeting all of us with hugs and kisses. But amongst these lovely children, not one adult was present.

A Brief Respite

We stayed in Sweden only a few hours before re-boarding the ship. A day or two later we docked in London, on March 29, 1946. The first thing I saw when I stepped off the boat was a truck passing by marked "kosher meat." It was a strange sight for me.

We were greeted at the docks by various Jewish organizations who knew in advance we were coming. Rabbi Schonfeld put us up in a beautiful luxury youth hostel at 32 Woodbury Down in NE London. Today it's a Muslim district; at that time, it was Orthodox Jewish. The rabbi hoped that bringing us back to a religious atmosphere would bring us back to Orthodoxy, but most of us were removed from the God we believed had failed us, even though we remained proud of our ancient heritage. We also became fiercely nationalistic about Palestine, repeating the phrase "Never Again!" to each other with fierce determination.

The good rabbi was funded by the religious/political party Agudat Israel, which was violently anti-Zionist at the time, believing Jews should not return to Palestine before the Messiah arrived. Given what we'd just lived through, coupled with the continuing Jewish struggles against the British in Palestine, most of us—especially the boys—wanted to go to the Holy Land. After three or four weeks, Rabbi Schonfeld gave all the males who had come to England on the SS Ragner an ultimatum: either study in one of his London yeshivas, or leave. We'd be on our own, able to do whatever we liked, but with no support from him or Agudat Israel. All the boys in my group decided we'd rather go on our own. Since we could no longer live in the hostel at Woodbury Down, eight of us rented a one-room apartment together and each went out to look for work.

I found a job as a fur cutter and bought a bicycle for about two pounds sterling. I rode it to work and back, buying sandwiches for lunch and meeting the other boys at the apartment for dinner. For the first time in a long time, I settled down to a relatively "normal" life.

London was delightful; in fact, I loved everything about England—the sites, the history, the people—until I visited the Old City, which was London's banking center, similar to New York's Wall Street. I was shocked and dismayed at the destruction inflicted by the Luftwaffe there. The Old City resembled what I'd witnessed in Warsaw, Berlin, and Dresden, and like Warsaw, one building stood intact: St. Paul's Cathedral. I'm sure the Germans didn't spare it because it was a cathedral; only luck allowed it to escape being flattened like the nearly two square miles around it.

I wanted to emigrate to the United States where my only remaining family lived, so I appealed to the Red Cross to find my mother's sister in New York. We made contact, but for whatever reason, she and my uncle were not at all cooperative. Perhaps my survival was too sharp a reminder of my parents' deaths and all the arguments and pain that grew out of their earlier decision to leave America. In any event, my relatives had a thirteen-year-old son who pleaded with my aunt and uncle to issue an affidavit for me to come to the United States—and so they did. I looked forward to thanking my cousin in person, but I never got the chance. He died of kidney disease a week before I arrived in America.

After filing my aunt's affidavit and many other documents in the US Consulate in London, I was informed I would have to wait a number of years before I'd be granted permission to enter the US under the Polish quota, established after the 1938 Evian Conference, and still in effect in 1946. I asked if I had to wait in England and was told no, that I could go anywhere; when the visa was approved, I could pick it up at any American consulate.

In the meantime, anyone who read the papers knew the situation was deteriorating in Palestine. The population of Britain was generally sympathetic to the plight of Jewish immigrants at that time, but the Foreign Secretary, Ernest Bevin, was an outright anti-Semite and was the man who had devised and issued the White Paper in the first place.

> For the Jewish refugees with Zionist convictions, who believed Zion was the only place where they would be both safe and fulfilled, Palestine was the obvious destination. Palestine was also the only practical option for most other Jewish refugees, Zionists or not, given the reluctance of Western countries at that time to resettle Jews. The only other option was repatriation to the countries from which the Jews had fled, an unacceptable option for the Jews. But the way to Palestine was blocked by the determination of the Arabs, and their ally, Britain, in their combined fight to resist transferring the international responsibility for the remnants of European Jewry to Palestine.[21]

In May 1946, the British Committee of Inquiry advocated terminating the 1939 White Paper and letting 100,000 European Jews into Palestine, but the Mandate Authority rejected their proposal. Bevin, in fact, is rumored to have answered Harry Truman's plea to allow 100,000 Jews into Palestine by saying the president only wanted them there so they wouldn't be on the streets of New York.

The three-way armed conflict between Arabs, Jews, and the English intensified in June 1946, when the British military raided the Jewish Agency in Palestine, confiscated thousands of documents, and subsequently arrested 2,500 Jews. It erupted into war the next month, when Menachem Begin's Irgun retaliated by bombing the King David Hotel, where the British military command and Criminal Investigation Division were headquartered. Although warning calls had been placed to the hotel, the French Consulate, and the *Palestine Post*, the British—as one official declared—"... don't take orders from the Jews."[22]

Consequently, ninety-one people were killed and forty-five more were injured.

Just one week later, the papers were filled with news of the worst post-war pogrom, which occurred in Kielce, Poland. Rioters —led by Polish soldiers and police officers and using as an excuse the paper-thin lie of a child told to avoid punishment—rounded up and summarily killed forty-one Jews, wounding fifty others. But the Poles didn't simply shoot them; they killed them with "sadism and bestiality."[23] This news "reminded the Jews of Palestine how Britain's restrictive immigration policy had condemned thousands to death."[24] It reminded those of us who had survived similar fates of the same thing.

I was one who got caught up in all of the news coming out of Palestine. I had joined a Zionist club in Golders Green, London, where I met some English youth, and we spent long hours talking about what was going on in Palestine and how war was inevitable. I found it incomprehensible that right after our recent catastrophe, my people should again face assured destruction even while the remaining survivors lingered in German refugee camps with no place to go. My resolve to help somehow, and perhaps in the process begin to exact a bit of revenge, took root.

Martin and friend Jack Pariser, Beuthen, Germany, 1945. Martin and the Parisers took refuge in this town to avoid danger in Poland.

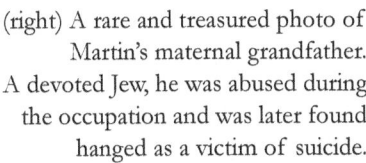

(left) The only remaining photograph of two of Martin's siblings: Necha (Nina) List, 1925-1943 and Jozef List, 1927-1943 Pilzno, Poland.

(right) A rare and treasured photo of Martin's maternal grandfather. A devoted Jew, he was abused during the occupation and was later found hanged as a victim of suicide.

(above) London, 1946. Day of arrival in England.
Martin is center left, dressed in black, with a dark bundle under his arm (the child to his right is carrying a white bundle).

(below) Another group shot of some of the boys transported to England after the war. Martin is pictured to the right of the boy carrying another boy on his shoulders.

In the Israeli army, 1948.

Tel Aviv, May 1948.
Martin and friend Haim Shermanski.
Here is where Martin finally began to physically grow again.

Guarding Jerusalem, Israel, 1948.

Martin and Haim Shermanski.
Israel, 1949.

Martin in Rome, 1949.

Graduation ceremony.
Martin is last on the right.

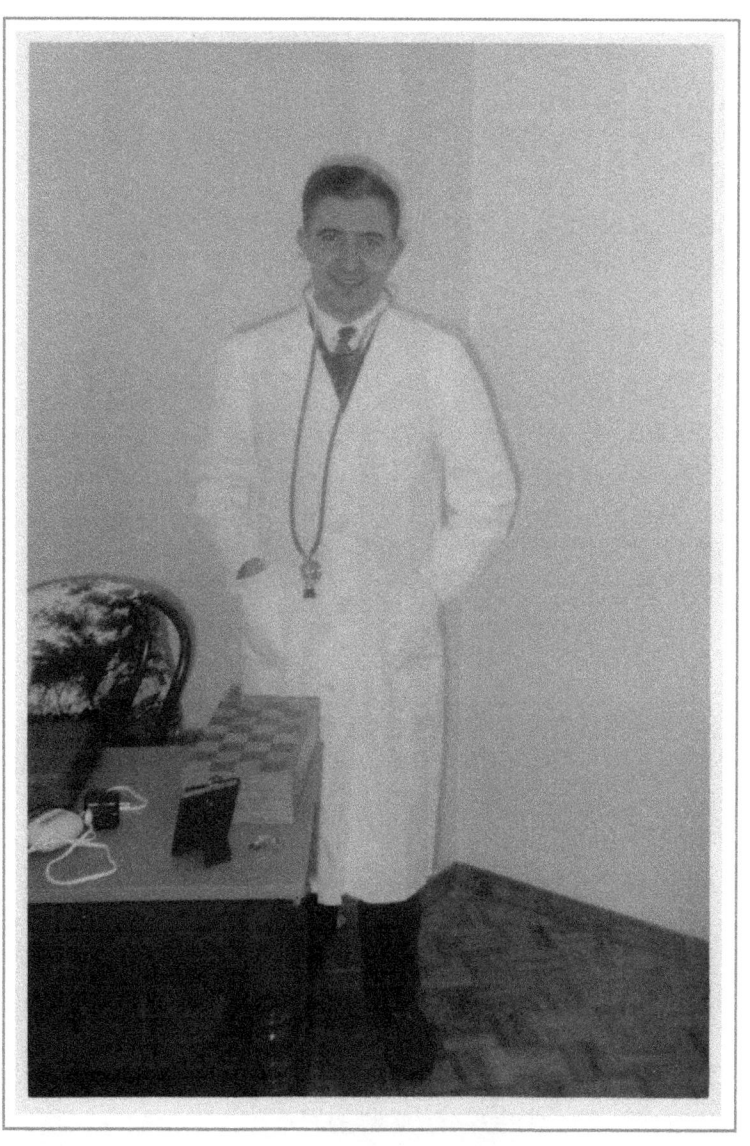

Dr. Martin List.
Bern, Switzerland, 1956.

(right) Martin List, Chairman of the Board, passport picture, 1985.

(below) Martin surveying for water at the Colorado Springs property, 1982.

(left) Monument established by the few Jewish survivors of Pilzno for family members. The names of Martin's father Leib List, brother Jozef List, and sister Necha List are engraved on the front.

(below) Alternate view of Jewish monument in Pilzno cemetery.

(above)
Joyful celebration with longtime friends,
Abraham and Sally Pariser, 1985.

(below)
Heritage Point, Mission Viejo, CA, 2009.

(left and below) Views from two different gates of the Jewish cemetery in Pilzno. Almost all tombs within were desecrated and memory stones stolen.

(below) Additional monument engraved in Hebrew in Pilzno's Jewish cemetery.

Last photo taken of Martin.
May, 2010.

9

FIGHTING IN PALESTINE

1947

In February 1947, just a few months after I turned seventeen, England decided to turn the Palestine Mandate over to the United Nations. This only increased my compulsion to go join the fight. I got in touch with the Jewish Agency on Bloomsbury Street in the West End of London and offered my services while awaiting my entry visa to the US.

My contact at the Jewish Agency, a member of the Haganah—the then-secret Jewish force in Palestine—said they were, in fact, looking for volunteers and asked how old I was. I knew I had to be at least eighteen to join the army, so I lied and said I was. It was almost true, but still not an easy fib to pull off: years of near-starvation had stunted my growth, and I still looked like a little boy. But I was determined, and they needed all the volunteers they could get.

With the Agency's help, I located David Davidovich in the KGB office in Berlin, a connection that would be very useful later on. I communicated with him and my Haganah contact primarily by phone until around the time the United Nations decided to partition Palestine into two states, one for the Jews and one for the

Arabs, at the end of 1947. Subsequently, I was advised to prepare to leave shortly, with directions to be provided as needed.

My contact said: "You will leave from Dover. Here's a ticket. A boat will take you across the channel to Oostende, in Belgium. Our agents will pick you up at the landing." He then handed me a photograph.

"This man will be on the boat with you. You and your fellow volunteers need to watch out for him. He will also board the same train you're taking to Paris. Make every effort to prevent him from reaching his intended destination. When you get to Paris, you will be met at the Gare de Lyon railroad station with further instructions."

So I packed my valise once again, said goodbye to my friends, and traveled to Dover. Unbeknownst to me, however, the agency's phone lines were tapped, and every bit of our conversation was known to British Intelligence, also known as MI5. Just as I was about to board the little boat with a group of other volunteers I recognized as fellow Holocaust survivors from Rabbi Schonfeld's youth hostel, I was approached by a civilian who flashed a badge at me: MI5.

"Martin List," he said. "Where are you going?"

I didn't even ask how he knew my name. I just answered, "Belgium."

"Belgium? Why Belgium?"

"Because I have an uncle there. I'm going to visit him."

The officer shook his head. "Look," he said, "don't lie to me. I know all about you. I know where you are going. You are going to Palestine. Let me tell you: you live in a country where you have every freedom. We will give you schooling. We will let you do whatever you want. Why do you want to go to Palestine where, I guarantee you, you will die?"

At that moment I knew he'd listened in on the conversation with my contact. Nevertheless, I kept insisting I was going to Belgium to visit my uncle. Finally he said, "Okay, have it your way. But remember, you will never be allowed to come back to Britain again."

I said I understood, boarded the boat, and left England behind in December 1947. As it turned out, the MI5 agent was right; I never did return to Great Britain. After fighting in Palestine and seeing Israel gain her independence, I wanted to go to London to say goodbye to my old friends before leaving for America, but when I went to the British consul in Rome, he already had a file on me. "We told you before you left," he said, "you will never go back to England. Never."

My group got to Oostende in four hours and boarded the train for Paris without incident. Some of my fellow volunteers noted the man in the photograph sitting in the train's bar having drinks with a Belgian woman. One took a seat on one side of the couple, another sat on the other side, and the rest of us mingled around, "inadvertently overhearing" their conversation. He was trying to impress the lady by telling her he was a senior officer in the British army on his way to serve under Glubb Pasha, commander of the Jordanian army. To our delight, he expounded on how he was going to "teach those bloody Jews some lessons." Making sure he did not reach his destination took on a new, special significance.

The woman became suspicious about my colleagues; she must have sensed some kind of imminent danger. When the man went to the bathroom, she asked that we not do anything in front of her.

When we parted company, my group trailed after the man into one compartment while she entered another.

As the train progressed toward Paris, the conductor came into our compartment to see our tickets. When he came back again about an hour later, he noted that one person was missing.

"Where is the other man who was in here with you?"

We shook our heads at each other and shrugged.

A Haganah agent met us at the Gare de Lyon station and accompanied us to the Gare du Nord railway station, from where we traveled that same night to Marseille. There, buses were waiting to take us to Trets, a village that was essentially an army training camp provided by the French. The French also provided a portion of the Marseille port for our use as needed. While training in Marseille, I resumed contact with David Davidovich. "Do me a favor," I said. "There are tons of German arms lying around all over Germany. Let me take some of them."

He readily agreed, on the condition we could find a way to transport them.

I told this to a French officer who said, "You need military trucks. We'll give them to you." They provided us with as many as we needed, which we used to ship truckloads of weapons from Berlin to Marseille, then packed onto ships that sailed to Palestine in defiance of the British-imposed embargo. With only me and my small group of volunteers, we worked to exhaustion one night moving arms from truck to ship.

Unfortunately, my KGB friend met a bad fate. He was eventually accused of being a Zionist agent. I don't know what his penalty was, but I hate to think what they did to him. To this day, I still feel terrible about losing him, especially to the enemy.

Like the Hurkovas, the French officers working with us were not doing all this because of their love of Jews. This was made clear in a conversation I overheard one day between a French officer and my commander. The officer said, "Is there anything else we can do for you?"

"No," my commander said, "but we are very grateful for your giving us this port and training facilities. But tell me, please, how come you are so nice to us?"

They were speaking English so I had no trouble understanding them, and I will never forget the French officer's answer: "No, we are not nice to you. We are repaying the treachery of the British for what they did to us. They took Syria and Lebanon from the Vichy government and promised to give them back after the war. They never did. So we are getting even with them by helping you.

The French army's payback merely strengthened my own quest for revenge, which, despite the few intervening years, was still as strong as ever.

I departed Marseille for Palestine on the Kedmah a few weeks later. Our ship was followed by the Egyptian navy in a threatening manner, so we set up machine guns on the deck, clearly visible to the officers and crews behind us. As such, we reached Palestine without incident. The British were preparing to depart Haifa but were still in charge of the port facilities and immigration control. I showed the customs officer my "tourist" visa.

"An awful lot of young Jews suddenly coming in as tourists," he grumbled. We were coming in by the hundreds, all with legitimate tourist visas. What could he do? He stamped our visas and let us off the boat.

I disembarked with the rest of the Haganah volunteers. Together with the Israelis waiting to meet us, we numbered a couple hundred people. Soon a man with a black patch over one eye, who I later came to know as Moshe Dayan, addressed us:

"I need one hundred and fifty volunteers. And I must warn you, you may never come back. I'll tell you later what it is, but who wants to volunteer? I would appreciate it."

I volunteered, along with most of the others with whom I'd arrived. We were immediately loaded onto a bus that took us to Kiryat Anavim, a kibbutz outside Jerusalem. There we were given munitions to carry on our backs and told to walk behind Arab lines to our objective, which was two buildings: the Hebrew University and the Hadassah Hospital. They were both on Mount Scopus, which was inside Jerusalem. Both buildings were completely surrounded by Jordanian Arab Legion forces. Mount Scopus was likewise surrounded. And so was Jerusalem.

Welcome to Palestine.

Under British rule in Jerusalem, Palestine, you could only build with Jerusalem stone, which is massive. The University was built of stone, but the hospital was built of ordinary cement. What that meant was, if someone fired a cannon at the University building, it bounced off like a ball; if they fired at the hospital, you were dead. Fortunately, I was assigned to the University.

The march behind enemy lines with heavy equipment on our backs took many hours, during which we were constantly exposed to detection by the enemy. When we finally arrived at our destination, we received a warm welcome from the two buildings' few defenders who pointed out the Jordanian army facing us from across from the University on Mount Olive.

Of the one hundred and fifty of us doomed to die in these two buildings, none was over eighteen, including me. Being wholly surrounded by the Jordanian Arab Legion, we were very tense. The United Nations had observers circulating between the combatants; our superiors told us that every one of the UN observers was either spying for them or for us. Having brought along new weapons, we proceeded to set up a machine-gun position facing Mount Olive. This did not escape the attention of the UN observers, one of whom immediately demanded an explanation from our commander, while threatening to report the change to his superiors. He was informed he must be suffering from optical illusions, that that position had not changed for a long time.

One of the volunteers, who brought a deck of cards, started a game of blackjack. We played around the clock in that tense atmosphere—individual players changed as they left for guard duty or fell asleep, but they were immediately replaced by others and the game went on and on, twenty-four hours a day. There was always one man on the lookout, peeking through a hole. He would periodically say, "They're coming at us," *they* meaning the Jordanian army led by the British General who had assumed the Arab name Glubb Pasha. The response to the lookout guy's announcement was always: "Don't disturb our game until they are in reach of our weapons."

We were using comparatively primitive weapons: German-made hand grenades with long handles that could reach twenty-five, maybe thirty yards depending on how good you were at throwing them, and homemade English sten guns that only had a range of about one hundred and fifty yards. There was no sense getting ready until the enemy was close enough to shoot.

The atmosphere of that blackjack game played with IOUs was so intense, you would be killed if you tried to cheat. Whenever the Arabs came close enough, we would utilize our weapons, then go right back to the game.

At one point, our officers ordered us to build fortifications using sandbags. Instead, we chose to use heavy books from the University library as protective shields. One day as I was piling up books on my position, the lone civilian academic who had managed to stay behind when the rest of the staff was evacuated came by. "Do you realize how precious those books are that you are destroying?" he demanded.

"Don't worry about any of that," I said. "None of us is going to get out of here alive."

He picked up a book from my top layer. "Do you have any idea who wrote this?"

I shook my head.

"It was written two thousand years ago by one Josephus Flavius. You should read it."

I took his advice; it was an amazing discovery for me. With the exception of the two buildings we occupied, the area had not changed in topography since the days when the book in my hands had been written. I could identify every detail as the author described how the Roman armies descended on Jerusalem two millennium earlier; it required no special training to clearly see the panorama unfold page by page. Flavius' narrative told how he eventually went to Rome in order to write the history of Judea's conquest by Roman forces, describing how the Roman emperor Titus had the Jewish leadership brought to him in chains. They were then paraded under the Arch of Titus in Rome, constructed to celebrate the defeat of Judea, the one country that dared resist the Roman empire.

It struck me that I had come full circle in understanding the real origin of the tragedy that befell us in the Holocaust. When I was in Rome some two years later, I climbed the Arch of Titus late one quiet night, and using a hammer and chisel, I inscribed in Hebrew on top of the arch: *Gam Zeh Nikachnu.*

This too we defeated.

The Jordanians never managed to displace us from the Hadassah Hospital or the University, which, in particular, stood as a symbol of our national pride. Eventually, an armistice was signed under which we, the defenders of Mount Scopus, were to be exchanged for a similar contingent of army units. As we assembled on the football field for the occasion, a delegation from the opposing side appeared in their Keffiyehs (headdresses). Their leader identified himself as none other than Glubb Pasha. Addressing our commander in English, he demanded we surrender our weapons before he would allow us to leave. Our officer translated that demand into Hebrew to our assembled unit; we all burst into laughter. "You just heard our answer," he said to Glubb Pasha. "And allow me to remind you, we are not your prisoners of war, but fighting soldiers. You attacked us; you never took those buildings. Now we have an exchange of personnel. People will come up with arms, people will go down with arms."

Thinking we did not understand his English, Glubb turned to his second in command and said, "What will these fucking Jews want next?"

We eventually made the exchange exactly as originally agreed. We went down with our arms; it would have been suicide for us to cross Arab-held territory without our weapons. But Pasha never knew we had already played a dirty little trick on him and the Jordanian Arab Legion.

The JAL had allowed oil to be brought up to us for heating that winter. We had radioed to the city, had the oil sent up in a barrel, and placed it right in the middle of an oil tanker, surrounded by much-needed weapons. When his truck pulled up to Mount Scopus, Glubb Pasha took out a stick and dropped it in the middle of the barrel, just as if he was checking the oil in a car. He lifted the stick, looked at it, and said, "Oil. Pass."

So the truck continued up the hill, leaving the oil we needed for heating along with the machine guns, mortars, and other weapons we needed for fighting Glubb Pasha and his JAL.

10

TRIUMPH AT ALL COSTS

1948

After coming down from Mount Scopus, I joined the Palmach, a division of the Haganah originally created in 1941 in conjunction with the British to help protect Palestine from the Nazis. More than just a military unit, the Palmach had been structured to foster a way of life that stressed agricultural and economic independence. Once the Allies stopped the Axis from gaining an African stronghold in 1943, however, the British ordered the Palmach dismantled. Instead, the Palmach went underground and became a model for the future Israeli army's commander-training program. Their training included small arms, munitions, sabotage, reconnaissance, and sniping along with physical fitness, Zionist education, agricultural training, first aid, and other essential instruction.

Having been trained before I got to Palestine and fulfilled my superiors' expectations on Mount Scopus, I was immediately accepted into the Palmach. During these months, now that I had sufficient food, I resumed growing, which had stopped while I was severely malnourished. Because of this the Army had to supply me every few weeks with new clothing appropriate for my height.

For the rest of my time in Israel, I had very little contact with anyone outside my army unit. I had no intention of becoming an Israeli; I was just a fanatical volunteer, fearless and ready to sacrifice myself after my suffering in the Holocaust. I hardly noticed the changes in climate and geography; my sole focus was winning the war. It meant everything.

One of my first assignments was unloading and opening crates of Czechoslovakian arms. Almost immediately after the UN partitioned Palestine on November 29, 1947, the US State Department declared an arms embargo that affected only the Jews, not the Arabs.

> As soon as the resolution passed, however, the State Department went to work systematically to undo it. The Palestine problem was dwarfed by the problems arising in Eastern Europe and the Mediterranean, where country after country was falling under Soviet influence. The US was demobilizing rapidly and had to decide whether to maintain a military footing to counter the USSR, and to face the possibility of another war, that would increase US dependence on Arab oil. Truman was deluged with memoranda about the situation in Poland, Czechoslovakia, and Greece, as well as with the Palestine question. The Presidential staff in those days was tiny, and Truman had to read each and every one of these documents.
>
> Palestine was a side show, so the State Department could act more or less independently in many ways, and despite official support for partition, most State Department officials remained opposed. On December 5, the US declared an arms embargo in the Middle East, which prevented the Jews from getting arms, but did not

affect contracts of the Arab states with Great Britain. The stand of President Truman on this embargo is unclear.[25]

I cried when I opened some of those crates and saw the beautiful machine guns we had so desperately needed during those long months on Mount Scopus. How had we gotten Czechoslovakian arms?

Czechoslovakia was at that time under communist rule, but curiously enough, the only time during the entire Cold War that the Soviet Union and America agreed on something was the partitioning of Palestine. Gromyko, USSR's foreign secretary, voted yes with the United States.

Stalin, hoping to create a communist base in what became Israel and knowing how desperate we were for arms, shipped us crates full of beautiful machine guns. My first was a German-made one known as an MG34, produced in the Skoda factory in Czechoslovakia, which the Germans ran during the war. How ironic that German machine guns made in Soviet Czechoslovakia would be used by Holocaust survivors to fight for a democratic Jewish homeland.

Sending us guns, however, was not simply an altruistic act. The Czechs desired to initiate a communist regime in Israel, so they allowed all the Jews in the Czech army to depart as one unit and go to Israel together. But the Israelis weren't stupid and immediately dismantled the unit, separating the men so they could not act as a united force.

When Stalin realized that this attempt to communize Israel failed, he put the leader of the Czech government, Rudolph Slánský, on trial for sending arms to Israel. Being the perfect scapegoat, Slánský knew he had no chance. He was convicted in

Prague and hanged for being a Zionist, even though he was actually a true, committed communist at heart. Writer Arthur Koestler attended that trial and patterned his famous *Darkness at Noon* Rubashov character on what happened in that Prague courthouse. *Darkness at Noon* was at least partially responsible for France not voting in a communist government in the first post-war elections.

A fascinating figure, Koestler was caught by Franco during the Spanish civil war when he was a correspondent for the London *Observer*. After the newspaper managed to convince Franco to release him, Koestler went to Britain where he was promptly imprisoned as an enemy agent because he was a German national.

Koestler was still a war correspondent for the *Observer* when the Arab-Israeli conflict broke out, and that's how I happened to meet him. A kibbutz called Ramat Rachel was in the middle of a village that had been captured by the Egyptian army. My unit was ordered to go in and "get rid of them." We entered in the early evening and found Egyptians feasting on chickens stolen from the kibbutz. We literally mowed them down in the dining room.

Having "gotten rid of them," my storm unit called up the regular army to come replace us, leaving the kibbutz in the hands of a unit of oldsters—or rather, an army unit of men too old to serve. We were on the way back to our base when they radioed: "The Egyptians came and took it back from us." We had to return once again and clean them out. By the time we got there, it was the middle of the night, and the remaining Egyptians were entrenched in the kibbutz's kindergarten. All of the children had already been evacuated, and we blew the whole thing up—kindergarten, Egyptians, and all. We might have been short of men and arms, but we had dynamite.

I was standing guard at dawn when a jeep appeared with two passengers: a man and a much younger lady. An avid reader, I immediately recognized Koestler from photographs in his books. He said, "Let me through."

"I'm sorry," I answered. "I know of you and I would love to let you through, but I have strict orders. No civilians."

He was furious. He swirled the jeep around and returned some twenty minutes later with a senior Palmach officer, who ordered me to let him in to see the field of battle. That was my only encounter with the famous writer.

I was part of many other operations during my volunteer service in Israel. We were not just fighting Palestinians; Jordanians, Egyptians, Iraqis, Syrians, and even Germans were also part of the melee. The Nazi factions were there as volunteers to help the Arabs kill us.; the others were more obsessed with the land and wanted the glory of grabbing Jerusalem. They succeeded, with the active help of the British, in grabbing the Jewish district of the old city. They killed most of its defenders, desecrated centuries-old synagogues by using them as horse stables for the occupying JAL, and denied any Jew access to pray at our holiest site, the Wailing Wall, which remained inaccessible to any Jew during the Jordanian occupation from 1948 until it was liberated in the 1967 Six-Day War.

An English nun named Miss Curry had established a nunnery on a hilltop just above an Arab village named Ein Karem. Today, Ein Karem is the site of Hadassah Hospital, one of Israel's largest. Millions visit it annually to view its world-renowned windows, the artistic creation of Marc Chagall. But in the fall of 1948, it was simply Ms. Curry's nunnery. Below it in Ein Karem sat the Iraqi army, having reached its western-most advance into suburban

Jerusalem, as well as forces of the Mufti of Jerusalem—Haj Amin El Husseini—who had spent the war in Berlin overseeing his Muslim SS command. Husseini's leader in Ein Karem, a Syrian Nazi named El Kaugi, led a gang that included Germans who had escaped trial in Germany only to be welcomed in Palestine as volunteers to help the Arabs kill us off.

One night, my unit assembled in Ms. Curry's nunnery, and shortly after midnight we descended on the collected Arab and European forces, taking them by total surprise. We killed most of them in hand-to-hand and bayonet combat, thus liberating Ein Karem.

I last saw that place during my 1987 sojourn to Israel, when I worked as a volunteer physician in Hadassah Hospital. The nunnery atop the hill was gone; nobody remembered its existence, much less its name. Nobody knew that this had been the westernmost point reached by the Iraqi Army in 1948.

After Israel became a state, all the divisions of the Haganah, including the Palmach became incorporated into the Israeli army. Not incorporated was the Irgun, a rival gang led by Menachem Begin. The Irgun were Jewish terrorists, the very type that had caused President Truman to write:

> I fear very much that the Jews are like all underdogs. When they get on top they are just as intolerant and cruel as the people were to them when they were underneath. I regret this situation very much because my sympathy has always been on their side.[26]

Triumph at All Costs

On the day Folke Bernadotte, a Swedish count appointed by the UN to attempt to broker a truce between the Jews and Arabs, was shot by a member of the Irgun, an officer addressed my company. "We just received orders to disarm these Jewish terrorists, the Irgun, on Mount Zion. If they refuse to surrender, you are ordered to shoot to kill."

Eight hundred of us were lined up to hear this. We all burst out laughing.

"What's so funny?" the officer demanded.

"Are you kidding," one of the men said. "You expect us to kill other Jews?"

"If you don't, I'm going to have you all court-martialed!"

"So be it."

An hour later he came back. "Modified order. Use whatever force you need to disarm them, but don't kill them."

We agreed to do that as we knew we could not be a state within a state, and the first man I fell upon in the attack happened to be Michael Barnet. When I grabbed his rifle, he said, "What the fuck do you want from me? First you machine gun me in the waters when I tried to reach you—and I'm not even Jewish!"

He was, in fact, English and had been a soldier in the British Eighth Army where he fought under General Montgomery. When he came back to England, he became engaged to a Jewess in London, who demanded he go assist the fighting in Palestine or she wouldn't marry him. He'd known nothing of the political infighting between Menachem Begin's Irgun and Ben Gurion's Haganah. The two groups were fighting each other for political power, almost like Hamas and the PLO, when Michael walked into the Irgun's Paris office.

Michael made the trip to Palestine on a ship called Altalena on which arch-terrorist Begin was transporting munitions and volunteers. When the ship came within approximately three hundred yards of the main beach in Tel Aviv and General Yitzhak Rabin torpedoed it under direct orders of Ben Gurion, Michael jumped ship and tried to swim to shore. He was machine-gunned in the water but survived, and he joined the Irgun when he recovered from his wounds. After our encounter on Mount Zion, he subsequently joined my unit.

One day during a fight with an Arab mob in the al-Shajara village of Jerusalem, we ran completely out of ammunition while hundreds of Arabs were coming toward us. I said, "Michael, it's time to run." But he was an experienced soldier and mocked: "Boy scout, boy scout" in response. After he sang his jingle, he picked up a barrel loaded with sand to protect us and rolled it down the hill toward the Arab mob. They assumed it was some kind of mega bomb and ran away by the hundreds, scattering in every direction. After that, he repeated his jingle, "Boy scout, boy scout." I learned a lot fighting alongside Michael and made a very good friend.

Back in November 1947, when the United Nations was hoping its two-state solution would solve the problem in the Middle East, about twenty young American Jews were studying medicine at the Hebrew University in Jerusalem, the very building I later defended. Right after Israel's independence the following May, Arab mobs surrounded a bunch of Jewish villages known as Kfar Etzion with the intent to destroy them. Ultimately they did, but not before those twenty American students volunteered to bring ammunition and food to those in the surrounded Kfar Etzion villages. The students never made it; they were captured in a village behind enemy lines and brutally slaughtered by the Arabs, who cut off their genitals and paraded them on sticks.

In November 1948, on the first anniversary of these young men's tragic deaths, Michael and I were part of the unit ordered to go into that same Arab village behind Arab lines and make retribution. Our orders were to kill everything that moved: men, women, children, even animals. We were fired up by a pep talk about what had happened to those American students, and the few hours' cruel march up and down hills to arrive at the village only made us more bloodthirsty. But when we descended, we found the village totally empty; there was no one to take our vengeance upon. Not to be dissuaded, we blew up all the local leaders' houses, decimating them. It felt good, but it hardly satisfied my personal quest for revenge.

One day Michael received a letter from his Jewish girlfriend in London telling him she had met someone else.

Horribly upset, Michael asked me to meet him for dinner that night in Tel Aviv, where he had some business to attend to. He showed me the letter when we met at the restaurant and claimed he could not live without her. I did my best to console him, but what did I know about affairs of the heart? At all of nineteen, I felt like I'd lived enough for two lifetimes and was certainly not a virgin, but none of my experiences had ever touched on this kind of situation. I lamely told him he'd probably feel better in the morning.

The next morning, the headline in what was then known as the *Palestine Post*—today the *Jerusalem Post*—said that Michael Barnet had been found dead on the beach from a self-inflicted gunshot. I was the only one who knew what motivated his suicide.

On February 24, 1949, Israel signed an armistice with Egypt, and for the most part, the fighting stopped. Lebanon signed with Israel on March 23, Jordan on April 3, and finally Syria on July 20, 1949. Being a volunteer, I asked to be discharged; shortly thereafter, in August 1949, I sailed to Italy.

11

BREATHING SPACE

1949

By the time I left Israel, my New York family—for reasons never disclosed to me—had sent me three thousand dollars, an astronomical sum for the times. That money, along with learning I could pick up my visa for the United States at any time, set my course of action. I immediately bought a tourist-class ticket on the Leonardo da Vinci, a new luxury ship that would get me to New York in four-and-a-half days. But I didn't leave right away. I felt I deserved a break from all the killing and horrors that had made up my life so far. I had my visa, my ticket, and money to burn —what more did a young man in Rome need?

I rented a *pensione* on Via Venezia, the same street the US embassy was on. It provided room and board, which left me plenty of money to spend—and I decided I would, in fact, spend every last dime before I left for New York. But first I needed permission to be in Rome for a period of time, so I went to the police station to get it.

"Why do you want to be here?" the officer asked.

"I've just survived a Holocaust and fought in a war," I said. "I want to live it up for a while."

"No," he said flatly. "I can't use that. You have to have a reason."

I looked at him, he looked at me. Finally he said, "Don't be sad," and he took me by the arm to the window. "See that building across the way? That's the Berlitz School of Languages. You go down there and tell them you want to study Italian culture. Then bring back the slip that says you're going to do that."

I brought back the slip, he stamped it, and I stayed in Rome.

My life was simple: I slept all day and went to nightclubs every night. For six months I celebrated the end of two wars by indulging in total debauchery with beautiful women. I had an intriguing accent and was young, fit, and good looking. They were gorgeous—oh, the women were gorgeous in Italy. I didn't know these women, so I of course took every precaution not to catch any diseases and to make sure I did not father any children. But I enjoyed life in Rome; it was a good thing I had already bought my ticket to New York or I might never have left.

The only serious action I took during my time there was that climb up the Arch of Titus. Otherwise, it was a time of *La Dolce Vita*—the sweet life—which I led until February 1950, when visa in hand, I finally boarded the Leonardo da Vinci in Genoa, Italy. Four days later I arrived in the land of opportunity.

As the da Vinci approached New York harbor, I reflected on my history. The memories of the Holocaust suddenly became very vivid. While in the forest, there had been constant discussions about the purpose of survival. Everyone always agreed the most important reason to stay alive was to exact revenge for the horrors inflicted on us. As the sole survivor of my extended family and one of the few left of my entire community—not to mention virtually all of Europe—I felt a heavy burden to avenge the barbarity of all those deaths.

The sight of the Statue of Liberty in all its glory and the majestic skyline of New York gave me deep pause as I sailed by; that memory remains with me to this day. I could hardly believe my luck at having arrived at this point in my life. Just twenty years old, I instinctively knew I had huge possibilities ahead of me. I had to make good in this new country—not merely for myself, but to honor my mother and father, my brother and sisters, my community, and the decimated Jewish people. I also instinctively knew that the key to my revenge lay within the borders of this amazing country.

My cousin Martha met me on the docks at pier fifty-two on the west side of Manhattan. It felt somehow strange to be in the company of a living relative. We took a cab to her business, a liquor store on Hudson Street in the village. Even after my experiences in London, Rome, and Israel, I was still agog at the crisscrossing highways and towers of Manhattan. The entire scene evoked the overwhelming sense that I had *arrived*, that unlimited opportunities awaited me here. My future, my revenge, my happiness—everything was possible here.

Martha's mother, my mother's sister, was waiting to greet me at the liquor store. Other aunts and uncles on my mother's side came by a few days later, waved hello, then ran as if I were a leper. They were all in the liquor business, but despite being wealthy, they were, for the most part, uneducated. I got the distinct impression I reminded them of their own humble origins. My mother's family had arrived in America at about the same time as my parents in the 1920s; my mother and father were the only ones who elected to return to their families in Poland. The others had stayed, built businesses, and now wanted nothing to do with anyone from "the old country." For that reason or maybe one I could not discern, my relatives were not friendly. I developed a sense of inferiority, as if there was some kind of shame attached to being a refugee, a Holocaust survivor. I was never invited to any of their homes. Occasionally they would take me to Horn & Harnet coffee house, for pie (ten cents) and coffee (a nickel). Beyond that, I was essentially someone to avoid, someone embarrassingly "old world."

I stayed with Martha and my aunt on Ninth Avenue and Fiftieth Street for about ten days, then found a job as a soda jerk and rented a room. As my public education had been terminated in the fourth grade, I intended to resume my studies without further delay. I knew education had to be my first priority in whatever lay ahead. Fortunately, I was already fluent in English, as well as four other languages—Polish, German, Russian, and Hebrew—and had more than a smattering of Italian. I was a quick study.

I enrolled in Washington Irving Evening High School and spent my days cleaning floors and windows on Wall Street for minimum wage, $1.20–$1.45 per hour, and my nights pouring over books. I soaked up the lessons like a sponge. My high school advisor told me I could take exams in any subject and if I passed, I would get credit for the entire course.

I became as single-focused on getting through school as I had been on staying alive in Pilzno. While working days to pay my rent on Manhattan's west side, I embarked on an intense, self-directed course of study at night, reading books as quickly as I could and taking exam after exam. Within two evening semesters, I had earned enough credits to obtain my high school diploma.

During my last week of school, I noticed an announcement on the school board about a scholarship competition. The New York

State Department of Education (NYSDE) would pay college tuition for anyone passing the examination. Needless to say, I jumped at the opportunity. A couple weeks after I successfully passed the exams, a Mr. Richman called me into the Manhattan office of the NYSDE.

"How long have you been in this country?" he asked.

"About a year."

"Then you're not a citizen, are you?"

"No, I have to be here five years to be a citizen."

"Then I don't understand. This competition is only for US citizens. Someone should have told you that you weren't allowed to take the examinations. Now because no one stopped you, we have a problem."

My heart sank; I had assumed this test would be my ticket to college. I could never afford to pay tuition on my meager earnings. Apparently, my disappointment showed because Mr. Richman picked up the phone right in front of me and called his superiors in Albany.

"I have this greenhorn in front of me who just got off the boat," he said. "He took the State Board examinations and passed them, because no one had informed him he was ineligible." He listened for a few minutes and then said something remarkable: "Look, this isn't right. No one told him he couldn't take them, no one stopped him when he showed up for the exams, and now he's passed. Are we going to make an exception and give it to him or do you want my resignation?"

When he hung up he turned to me and said, "Go home. You'll hear from us in a few days."

Indeed, a few days later I received a letter stating that an exception was being made in my case and that I would receive a tuition scholarship for four years of college provided I maintained a B average.

I applied to Columbia University and was overjoyed at my good fortune when I got accepted. It seemed that I, unlike the rest of my family, had been born under a lucky star. I still needed money for room and board, so I took a night job working in drugstores on the east side of New York. My boss had a special dislike for students, so I could not reveal to him why I was always coming to work five minutes past six. The truth was, my class ended at five minutes till, making it nearly impossible to be on time. He would stand in the doorway looking at his watch as I approached, shaking his head in dismay.

Most of my classmates did not have to work their way through school; in fact, I felt rather strange in the midst of that crowd of students from wealthy families. Here I was a refugee from the forests of Poland, cast amongst the richest kids in America—the elite. At twenty-one, I was also already a couple of years older than the other freshmen and had experienced much more life than they could have imagined. All they were worried about were fraternity parties, cars, and girls; all I was worried about was getting an education. I never felt like I really belonged there.

Across the street from Columbia was Barnard, an elitist school for girls. I met Marcia Zwanger from Barnard one day and before long, I fell madly in love with her. She was from a fairly rich family in Queens, however, and they detested me for my poverty. They thought their daughter was the perfect Jewish princess, too good to be entangled with a refugee Holocaust survivor. They particularly resented my taking her out by subway, not realizing how difficult it was for me to have the ten-cent fare for both of us. Her father threatened to intervene in the State Department and have me deported to Poland—which, of course, he could not do—while her brother told me, "If you truly love my sister, let her go. You're not in her class." I was heartbroken when she decided to break off our romance, but it only made me all the more determined to continue my studies. Once again I remembered that the reason I had survived, the very *purpose* of my survival, was to take revenge.

Years later, after I had become a physician, I worked in Long Island Jewish Hospital where, unbeknownst to me, Marcia's brother was a radiologist. We met in a lecture conference one day. Seeing my white coat and stethoscope, he said, "Martin, now that you're a doctor, you must call Marcia. Let me give you her telephone number in San Francisco." Shortly after that I was sent, all expenses paid, to present a lecture on medicine at the Mark Hopkins Hotel in San Francisco. I called Marcia, and she immediately came to meet me, offering to drive me to her luxurious home in Marin County.

Our discussion on the trip to her house made me wonder what I had ever seen in the girl. She had turned into a hippie—a flower child—and was spouting socialism. Before we reached the Golden Gate Bridge, I politely asked her to take me back to the Mark Hopkins Hotel because I knew we were no longer compatible. She turned the car around and took me back. I never saw her again.

I continued to date many beautiful girls in New York. Most wanted a stable relationship, but I was not ready for anything like that at the time; medical school was my foremost objective. I would take them to select cafés on the East side of Manhattan, or for brunch at the Tavern on the Green in Central Park. We would rent a boat for two and go rowing for hours on the lake. Sometimes we'd go to Bradley Beach in New Jersey, which was my favorite.

I tended to date girls who were exceptionally desirable and intellectual. Some I took home to my rented room near Columbia and engaged in lovemaking. I cherish those memories even today, but alas, my plans left no room for relationships. I enjoyed life to its fullest extent, but my heart and soul were preoccupied with retribution and the education I needed to exact it.

I was particularly drawn to the subjects of pharmacology and toxicology—especially the binary gasses being discovered by refugee German scientists working at Columbia—as well as other biological poisons. One biochemistry professor named David Nachmansohn—a former student of Nobel Prize Winner Otto Meyerhof—worked at Columbia during the war creating these binary gasses. One gas used alone was harmless; two in combination became a deadly weapon. Such a combination was actually used on one occasion in the Tokyo subway years later by some disgruntled Japanese group, with horrible results.

I elected to major in pharmacology—all part of my brewing maniacal scheme to singlehandedly poison millions of Germans. I shared my ideas with no one; this would be my personal act of retribution for all that had been done to us. I went about it methodically and scientifically. I was indifferent to any and all consequences and had total contempt for the resulting public opinion. Looking back, this insane plotting and daydreaming of revenge was almost therapeutic because it kept me from falling apart. Time did not matter; I was young and knew I needed careful preparation. Hence, I talked to Professor Nachmansohn about the "how" of his work, never indicating my purposes. He provided guidance to his papers on the subject, which I studiously absorbed.

I decided to perfect my studies of these materials by enrolling in medical school once I graduated from Columbia. I was, however, stymied by three things: one, my financial position was not conducive to such an undertaking; two, my mother's family was utterly disinclined to help (their attitude was, "We brought you over here, now you're on your own!"); and three, it was not easy for a Jew to get into medical school in America in those days. Medical schools practiced *numerus clausus*: restriction of the number of Jews. How did they know who we were? Very simply: at the bottom of the application you had to include a letter from your clergyman. That made it easy to tell who the Jews were.

By the time I graduated, I'd been in the United States for six-and-a-half years. Although I was focused on my studies, I had not stopped paying attention to what was going on with Jews around the rest of the world. While American medical schools were restricting us from becoming doctors, "the 1950s found Iraq's government leading a series of joint Arab military campaigns to wipe out Israel."[27]

Jews had peacefully lived in Iraq—known in the Bible as Babylon, Land of Shinar, and Mesopotamia, and said to be the location of the original Garden of Eden—for 2,700 years. After Israel won its independence, Jews began emigrating out of the now Arab Iraq to other countries. Many of those who did not go to Israel went to Iran, where, at the time, the Persians considered themselves above the rest of the Arab culture and had no problem with Jews. The Iraqi government, however, in retaliation for the Arab-Israeli war, declared in 1950 that Zionism was a capital crime and prohibited any more Jewish emigration. It was Germany, 1933, all over again.

> [L]ike all popular laws … [this] was aimed at cracking down on terrorism, but really just gave everyone an excuse to harass and abuse an unpopular domestic element. In this case, the law increased persecution of Jews. After intense negotiations aimed at rescuing Iraqi Jewry from further torment, the Israeli government negotiated a one-time airlift in 1951, called Operation Ezra. The émigrés had to leave most of their wealth behind—but it was probably going to be confiscated anyway if they stayed.[28]

By the time I left for my first semester of medical school in Switzerland, there were only about six thousand Jews left in Iraq. Following in Hitler's footsteps, the Arabs eliminated the Jewish culture almost everywhere in the middle east, except in Israel and Iran. It took the 1978 Islamic Revolution to get rid of the last of the Jews in Iran. By then, Jews had been expelled or had fled for their lives from almost every country in the Middle East—usually having left their land and possessions behind.

12

CHANGE OF HEART
1956

I worked as a soda jerk in Far Rockaway, Long Island, the summer after I graduated Columbia, frequenting those lovely beaches every chance I got. I met many girls, but they were all looking for husbands and I was determined to remain single due to my financial situation.

That year, Yeshiva University opened its first class in medicine. I found the ten dollars to apply and was asked in for an interview. Finding my qualifications acceptable, my interviewer demanded to know how much money I could contribute to the new school. Taken aback, I said, "None."

"Then how do you plan to pay for your tuition?"

"I'll manage," I assured him.

"How?"

"I'll manage," I repeated.

"Sorry, we cannot accept you," he said.

Here I was, probably the only Holocaust survivor to ever apply there, in that rich Jewish city of New York, but they had no room for the likes of me. The incident left me with a bitter resentment. I had no more money for applications—every application cost ten dollars—and I'd just become a US citizen, but because I spoke German fluently and knew I could go to a European school for free, I decided to leave the US. I did not want to go to Germany to study so I chose the University of Bern in Switzerland, a state school where I could take advantage of government-paid tuition. My classmates would be mostly Swiss, so language was no barrier. All I had to do was earn enough money to subsist through each school year.

I traveled by ship to Bern and met with the dean, a German who had escaped Germany to teach in Switzerland. He asked me why I wanted to study medicine.

"I have no intention to ever practice medicine," I said. "I'm just here out of scientific curiosity."

"Really? You're the first applicant I've ever seen who isn't out to save the world!" With that, he stamped my application and I was in.

I immediately concentrated on the Bacteriology Department to continue working on my revenge plans with a foremost focus on anthrax and botulism. This absorption in a school that employed quite a few German instructors had unforeseen consequences. For one, Professor Hildebrand, a "good" German who had escaped to Switzerland to avoid serving Hitler, became somewhat suspicious of my great interest in destructive agents. Another professor, Dr. Von Muralt, a Swiss physiologist who was barred from teaching at Yale after the war due to his pro-Nazi activities during the war, had the good grace to recuse himself from administering my exams, especially after he learned I was a survivor. He had his assistant substitute for him.

At some point, one of my Swiss classmates introduced me to his sister, an exceptional beauty of movie-star quality. Intellectually, however, we had nothing in common. Her family owned much of the city of Bern. One night, she asked me why I had never asked her to marry me. "Could it be because I'm not Jewish?" she asked. Before I could respond, she added, "I want you to know we had better Jews in our family than you."

"Like who?" I asked.

"My mother's sister was married to Albert Einstein when he worked in Bern," she said, her nose rising ever higher. We broke up shortly after; I found her intellect sterile. Her brother never spoke to me again.

I lived frugally in Bern, earning a little money and free living space by teaching German to some American students. Coffee houses in Bern are unique. For about twenty-five cents I could sip a coffee at my own reserved table, where I could read the international newspapers they had available for the clientele. On Sundays I would go to the Hotel Belvedere (where all spies met—I got to know some), sit on the balcony, and read the London *Observer* and the European edition of the *New York Herald Tribune*, very popular with American expatriates in Europe and still published in Paris.

At the end of every term, I returned to New York to make some money as a busboy in the Catskills so I could get through another school year. All the Jewish yentas were on the lookout for prospective husbands for their daughters, and I was almost a good catch—except that I had no money and was totally dedicated to my pursuit of biological-warfare revenge on the entire German nation.

While in Switzerland I met Heidi Wyss, a fellow female student who happened to be a German Protestant. Before long, we had fallen head-over-heels in love with each other. Her father had been in the SS during the war, and she told me how she hated him for the things he told her he had done. "The new German generation detests what our country did to the Jews," she said. And she was no phony.

Eventually, as her unconditional love and affection healed many of my wounds, Heidi became my life above all. Gradually, the folly of my deadly plans dawned on me. In essence, I was plotting to kill people just like Heidi, who had nothing to do with the actions of her parents. She was totally accepting of me; I had never experienced such complete and unqualified love. I learned to draw a distinction between the young German generation and their forebears.

One day in the pediatric lab, our exercise was to take a drop of blood from our finger and examine it under our microscopes. Suddenly, Heidi screamed. I rushed to her desk. "Look at my slide," she said in tears. I looked; the blood sample showed that she had the most virulent form of Leukemia, for which there was no cure at the time.

When Heidi died three months later, part of me died with her. Some four years later, I found myself working at Sloan Kettering Cancer Institute researching that very disease with my colleagues. We found no cure, but we did help develop methods to arrest it for some time. Today it is curable, but it sadly came too late for Heidi.

One day in my senior year at the University of Bern, Professor Rossi, chairman of the pediatrics department, was lecturing on the problems of infectious diseases and demonstrated a child dying of an infection resistant to all forms of (then known) antibiotics. "Nothing more can be done for this child," he concluded. "I predict the child will die within the next twenty-four hours."

Change of Heart

I left the lecture hall saddened by what I had witnessed and, as was my habit, went immediately to the adjacent library where I picked up *Lancet*, a British medical journal, to catch up on some reading. Glancing through the pages, I noticed an article describing a newly discovered analog of penicillin produced in England that was capable of destroying resistant forms of bacteria.

I rushed back to Professor Rossi with the journal, excited about the potential cure for his just-presented case. He heard me out with a stern look on his face. When I finished telling him about the new discovery, he said, "If you think you're so smart, why don't you get this medicine?"

I didn't have the money to call the manufacturer in London, but I managed to borrow it from a fellow student. The person I spoke to was very helpful. "I'm sending the medicine in the morning. Meet the pilot at the airport, and he'll hand it to you personally."

"I asked the cost and was told, "No charge."

The next morning I rushed the vial to Professor Rossi, who accepted it with some contempt but nonetheless administered it immediately to the sick child. The next day, he demonstrated to our class how the child had experienced a miraculous recovery within the last few hours following the intake of a newly discovered antibiotic. He never mentioned my role in discovering or obtaining the medicine; nevertheless, I felt triumphant in having saved the life of a beautiful child.

I finished my medical studies at University of Bern in December 1961 and returned to the United States. By then, I had dropped my insanely evil plans and decided to embark on a real medical career, realizing that my focus on toxicology and pharmacology was ideally suited for work in cancer and blood diseases, where such knowledge was particularly useful.

Ultimately, that decision proved to be one of the best I ever made. There are moments in a physician's life that bring an indescribable joy to those who have never experienced the magic of knowingly saving a human life. One such moment occurred for me years following my postdoctoral studies while I was practicing hematology and oncology at Hoag Hospital in Newport Beach, California. I was brought in to consult on a four-year-old girl who was bleeding profusely and required an immediate transfusion to survive the next twenty-four hours. Her family, who were Jehovah Witnesses, refused to allow me to transfuse their child as it was contrary to their religious beliefs. I called upon their minister to help me persuade them of the inevitability of their child's impending death, but they stubbornly refused. Because she was a minor, I chose to take the issue before a judge in night court, who immediately granted me a court order to proceed. Consequently, the child survived.

There have been innumerable such moments over the span of my medical career that made my studies and work memorable and extremely gratifying. On the other hand, there have also been moments of profound sadness. One night during my second year of residency, the workload in the Beth Israel Medical Center Emergency Room in New York became exceptionally heavy. The only ones on duty were my supervisor, Dr. Friedman, and I, and the two of us were overwhelmed with critically sick patients, most suffering from heart attacks. Dr. Friedman urged me to form a triage system, instructing me to ignore those not likely to survive and concentrate on those who could be saved.

I recall one patient struggling for breath while I attempted to alleviate his condition. Dr. Friedman came over, took one look at the patient, and said: "This one's not savable. Go on to the next." As he turned away, he added, "Oh, by the way, that's my uncle."

Nineteen-sixty-one was a year of both triumph and dismay for those of us watching the timeline of modern anti-Semitism. The same month I graduated medical school, Adolf Eichmann, the administrator of Hitler's Final Solution, was found guilty in an Israeli court for his role in murdering over a million Jews and sentenced to be hanged. Yes, although my quest for revenge had by then been tempered by Heidi's love, still I felt no small sense of satisfaction in the verdict and eagerly awaited his execution in May of the following year.

But his death did nothing to end the ongoing hatred of Jews, nor did it temper the dissemination of lies about the Jewish religion, people, and culture. Nineteen-sixty-one was also the year that Syrian Minister of Defense Mustafa Tlass wrote a book "explaining" that the blood libel [the accusation that Jews made ritual Matzo by slaughtering Christian children and using their blood] is really a fact, and that the Damascus accusation of 1840 was justified. This triumph of intellectualism has been reprinted many times in Syria."[29]

I arrived back in the United States in January 1962, found myself a motel room, and took the New York State medical license exams.

Then, just to be on the safe side, I did the same thing in Connecticut in case I might eventually set up my practice there. Internships at that time offered room and board but no salary. I signed up to do my internship at Long Island Jewish Hospital, but it did not start until July, so I had six months to explore other ideas.

I decided to explore them in California and obtained a "drive-away," meaning I drove someone's car to San Francisco for them. They paid for gas, food, and motels, along with giving me a few extra dollars on the side. Once I'd delivered the car, I got a motel room and set out to take the California medical license exam. When I passed, I had license to practice medicine in three states.

I liked California. Rather than return immediately to the East Coast, I obtained a so-called externship at Mount Zion Hospital working in their cardiac catheterization lab. For the next six months, I roomed with Oliver Sachs in a little cubicle with two bunks. Oliver was just finishing his internship at Mount Zion and spent much of his time lifting weights in his attempt to win the West Coast heavyweight competition. He had to put on a lot of weight for the competition; when we both left at the end of June, the hospital administrator remarked, "I expect the hospital's food bill will decrease substantially now that Dr. Sachs is leaving."

Oliver had a motorbike and took me frequently to his hangouts, one of which was a famous bookstore called City Lights, run by a well-known Buddhist who always gave us coffee and let us browse through his books. It was the age of the hippies/flower children, centered mostly in a district known as Haight-Ashbury. I did some unpaid volunteer work in a clinic there in my occasional spare time; the hippies had all kinds of weird diseases, mostly venereal.

When I decided to return to New York, I rode part of the way back on Oliver's motorbike. At one point we were running out of gas and asked someone where the nearest gas station was. "Bakersfield," we were told. When we arrived there, Oliver pulled his diary out of a hippie leather bag he was carrying and wrote: "Bakersfield, CA. There is no Bakersfield."

From there, we split in different directions: I hitchhiked to New York and Oliver went on to make vital contributions in the treatment of Parkinson's and encephalitis lethargica, which he described in his book *Awakenings*, later made into a movie of the same named directed by Penny Marshall and starring Robin Williams and Robert DeNiro.

I arrived in New York on July 1, 1962, just in time to start my internship. That very first week of July, the interns and residents at Bellevue City Hospital in Manhattan staged a strike, refusing to work for just room and board. Capitulating, the hospital granted them one hundred dollars per month.

Long Island Jewish Hospital decided to add this salary to its intern/resident contracts as well, so I was rich! I bought a very old Cadillac for eighteen dollars, taught myself to drive it, and took off to Manhattan cafés when I got my monthly pay. Intern hours were long and exhausting—we worked thirty-six hour shifts with twenty-four hours off—but after sleeping all through my "off" day, I found myself in nightclubs come evening.

My family was very proud of their "nephew the doctor," but we had little contact; in fact, we had total estrangement. Just as before, I received not one invitation from anyone for any event or holiday. Occasionally, when I drove into Manhattan, one aunt would invite me to Lindy's on Broadway for their famous cheesecake and coffee, but that was it. Looking back, I cannot help but feel that the loss of my immediate family, followed by the disregard and dismissal from my extended family—along with the loss of my young love in Switzerland—set a pattern in my life. I never married, and I never felt the "call" of family. I long ago became not only comfortable but content with my own company.

But I did very much enjoy the company of intelligent and beautiful women, and it was not long before I became somewhat friendly with one of my female colleagues, which certainly helped relieve tension at appropriate intervals of our work.

A few months into my internship, we were given a week's vacation, which my lady friend and I took by flying to Florida and staying at a resort hotel. It was a pleasant break from our high-pressure work, until we were driving our rental car slowly along the beach when a drunken sailor crashed into us, flipping our car across four lanes of highway. Fortunately, I had insisted we put on our seat belts just a few minutes earlier; as a result, we both walked away unharmed. The insurance agent offered us two thousand dollars each, but we vehemently refused to take the money, since neither of us was injured. Despite the accident, we enjoyed the rest of our vacation before returning to the rigors of our internship in New York.

13

ENLIGHTENMENT BEYOND EDUCATION

1963-1967

As my internship progressed, I elected to continue to specialize in internal medicine and arranged to commence my residency at Beth Israel Medical Center on First Avenue and Sixteenth Street in Manhattan on July 1, 1963, one day after finishing my internship. The work at Beth Israel was equally as hard and the hours just as long as at Long Island Jewish Hospital, but being in the city at least provided the advantage of nightlife. I was still living in residents' quarters in the hospital, but whenever I had a moment of freedom, I could continue my chosen lifestyle in New York City's myriad nightclubs.

Many of the Beth Israel staff doctors were wealthy and would have me take their night calls for patients on Park Avenue or Fifth Avenue—both affluent areas—and keep all fees for the work. I earned two to three hundred dollars a week from this temporary arrangement, which afforded me a robust social life.

One night I took such a call to attend to a member of the famous Astor family. I received the call late and arrived after midnight to find the lady of the house intoxicated. As I started examining her she said, "You're Jewish, aren't you?" Then she slapped my face—she had a very strong arm for someone so drunk. I ignored the insult and the assault and gave her an injection of sedative, but her family was embarrassed and apologetic. I told them to make nothing of it since she was obviously not cognitive of her actions. When I asked for my usual fee of twenty-five dollars for the house call, one of the family members said, "Oh no, that's not right!" as he stuffed money into my coat pocket. I pulled out the bills during the cab ride back to the hospital; they had put five hundred dollars in my pocket. Oh, was I rich! My café nightlife improved even more.

The post-doctoral period is not an easy one, as anyone who studies medicine knows, but I managed to procure positions at some of the best institutions. After two years of residency, I got a year-long fellowship specializing in blood diseases at Mount Sinai Hospital under Dr. Dameshek, a world-renowned hematologist, followed by another year-long fellowship at Sloan Kettering Institute, which to this day is the main temple of cancer research under the tutelage of Dr. Karnofsky, the "Father" of oncology.

While there, I and another fellow—the son of one of the men who founded American Express—concentrated on leukemia research. We were extreme opposites on the financial spectrum—he was very wealthy, I was eking along on my meager salary—but we were both very passionate about solving childhood leukemia. Together we got a grant from the Rockefeller Foundation to do work on the weekends. Though we didn't find a cure, we made some very nice discoveries in the process that allowed us to prolong the lives of children, at least for a few years.

Enlightenment Beyond Education

When our grant expired in 1967 and we needed more money to continue the research, we were called in before the Rockefeller Foundation board. "Gentlemen," they said, "we gave you money. What results do you have?"

My partner and I were taken aback. "You cannot do research on a day-to-day basis. It takes years. Give us a little more money and we will continue to work."

The board's decision was swift and unanimous: "You got your chance. No more money."

That rejection was a turning point in my life. I realized I could not rely on others for money if I wanted to pursue academic research. I was thirty-eight years old, out of medical school for six years, and still making only a couple hundred dollars a month. Where other men my age had wives, children, homes with equity, and nice cars, I was too absorbed in my work for anything other than a series of casual girlfriends. I lived on such meager earnings that I could not rise above an efficiency apartment, and I drove around in a little Rambler held together with scotch tape, my ancient Cadillac having long since bit the dust. I had nothing to hold me in New York; my family and I could not have been more estranged if we had never met. Clearly, it was time for a change.

In short order, I left Sloan Kettering, packed up my precious few belongings once again, and took off in my little Rambler for California, where I knew the weather was better and, I hoped, the medical and financial opportunities.

Throughout the long period between my finishing medical school and leaving New York for California, the global sentiment had not changed much from the days when the British blockaded Palestine against the Jews. In 1960, Israel Foreign Minister Golda Meir challenged Arab leaders in the United Nations General Assembly to negotiate a peace settlement with Israel's Prime Minister, but Gamal Abdel Nasser reiterated that Egypt would never recognize, much less negotiate, with "the Jewish State." Between 1963 and 1964, the Arab League I had fought against in the Palmach introduced a new division: the Palestine Liberation Organization (PLO), meant to be "a Palestinian nationalist umbrella organization dedicated to the establishment of an independent Palestinian state," whose charter specifically called for Israel's destruction.[30] As Nasser told the United Arab Republic National Assembly: "The danger of Israel lies in the very existence of Israel as it is in the present and in what she represents."[31]

The history of the Arab people is laden with factions and this new group was no exception; Yasser Arafat's Fatah soon came to dominate the PLO, which concentrated on guerrilla attacks on Israeli civilians throughout 1965, 1966, and the first four months of 1967. But the PLO was not alone; Syria reacted to Israel's National Water Carrier, which facilitated farm irrigation in the region for the first time in history, by shelling Israeli farms and villages. The UN refused to do anything to stop the Arab attacks but was quick to condemn Israel for its own retaliation, thus supporting Nasser's contention that "We shall not enter Palestine with its soil covered in sand; we shall enter it with its soil saturated in blood."[32]

Arab attacks against Israel were supported financially and with arms by the Soviet Union, which had been trying to eradicate all religion, including Judaism, since the Communist revolution in 1917.

> Russia competed with the US to be the first to recognize the infant Israeli state in 1948—only to switch later to all-out

support of the Arab quarrel against Israel. Today [1958] the 3,000,000 Jews who still live in Russia are warned to merge themselves completely in Soviet society (while still carrying documents designating them as Jews) and are discouraged from their own cultural identity.[33]

Khrushchev complained that "Soviet Jews preferred intellectual pursuits to such 'mass occupations' as the building trades and metal industry,"[34] but nevertheless asserted that "the road is open and no problem exists for Soviet Jews who might want to leave for Israel," prompting a dramatic increase in visa applications, especially from Jews in the Baltic states in 1965-66.[35] The Soviet government's leniency toward Jewish emigration to Israel, however, came to a virtual halt with the June 1967 Six-Day War, in which the Soviets, again, provided weapons and financial support to the Arabs.

> The armies of Egypt, Jordan, Syria, and Lebanon are poised on the borders of Israel ... to face the challenge, while standing behind us are the armies of Iraq, Algeria, Kuwait, Sudan and the whole Arab nation. This act will astound the world. Today they will know that the Arabs are arranged for battle, the critical hour has arrived. We have reached the stage of serious action and not declarations.[36]

Iraqi President Abdul Rahman Arif spoke for those Arabs when he said, "Our goal is clear—to wipe Israel off the map."[37] The aggressors' forces numbered approximately 465,000 troops, over 2,800 tanks, and 800 aircraft, all poised to attack and annihilate less than two million Jews, most of whom were civilians.

As history shows—and in this instance not even the most virulent anti-Semites contest—on June 5, the outnumbered, outgunned Israeli forces outmaneuvered the Arab world to the point that both the United States and the Soviet Union were concerned about Israeli troops marching on the capitals of Egypt, Syria, and Jordan. On June 10, Israel agreed to a cease-fire, having already accomplished its objective of capturing the Sinai and Golan Heights and defeating its "Goliath" enemies. In the end, Israel suffered 777 deaths with 2,586 wounded while the mighty Arab forces lost 15,000 Egyptians, 2,500 Syrians, and 800 Jordanians. I was beyond proud; my Holocaust survivor oath of "Never Again" had been picked up and reinforced by a new generation of Zionists.

But though we won the war, the battles not only continued, but expanded. Nineteen sixty-seven was also the year that an elderly liberal Catholic Cardinal—who had participated in the Second Vatican Council and should have known better—helped kick off the Holocaust Denial that so many anti-Semites now rally around. In an interview with a Los Angeles rabbi, Cardinal Frings of Cologne, Germany, stated that the Jews had been too economically powerful in the 1920s, doubting that six million Jews were actually killed under Hitler.[38]

After driving my Rambler across the country to Southern California, I stopped at a gas station. "How do I get to Newport Beach?" I asked the attendant.

"Stay on this street and drive two more miles," he said. "If you hear a splash, you've gone too far."

I checked into a motel near the beach, then went the following day to see Dr. Richard Opfell, the only oncologist in the county.

"I just got to Orange County, and I'd like your advice," I said. "I have no idea about the area. Where would you suggest I set up my practice?"

Dr. Opfell was very friendly. He asked me where I'd trained, and we chatted for awhile. Then he picked up the phone and called my former chief of staff at Sloan Kettering. After he finished his discussion, he reached into his pocket, took out a bunch of keys, and tossed them to me.

"I haven't had a vacation in ten years," he said. "Here's my offer: you take over my practice while I go out of town and get some rest. Then when I come back, I'll help you set yourself up." I readily agreed, and we subsequently became good friends. Richard was an excellent doctor, devoted to taking care of his patients.

There were a number of hospitals in the county. When Richard returned from vacation, he and I decided to split them up, each of us visiting half of the hospitals every day to ensure we were providing adequate specialized care. Dividing the county geographically, we agreed neither of us would retire for the night until every hospital had been covered for the day. I opened my office next to Hoag Hospital in Newport Beach that July, just a month after the Six-Day War, and quickly became known as a Doctor's Doctor. My colleagues were very friendly and my practice grew quickly from their referrals, but they liked to poke fun at me for hanging onto my little Rambler. "Doctors don't drive such cars," they said. Just to spite them—for some reason I had become proud of my humble background—I kept driving it.

Besides being a flagship hospital in Orange County, Hoag also had a nursing school. Although I remained keenly focused on my work, when playtime came, it was refreshing to find company in the beautiful young nursing students. But, as usual, the bulk of my hours were dedicated to work, and I wasn't interested in any permanent relationships.

I instructed my office assistants that I would see any indigent person seeking help free of charge, but I quickly discovered there were hardly any indigents in Newport Beach, a community known for its wealth. Nor were there many poor students on campus at University of California, Irvine (UCI), where I volunteered to teach twice a week. As my practice grew, so did my income, affording me the opportunity to buy a beautiful home right on the beach in Corona del Mar, just four miles from my office. Eventually, I even broke down and bought a Rolls Royce to replace my tired old Rambler. In fact, I bought two. Whether it was a reaction to all those years of poverty or simply a celebration of the change in my fortune, I began thinking of money in an entirely different way. As I continued to make large bank deposits, I even began accumulating an art collection. I was not going to "live poor" any longer.

One day the manager at my bank wanted to talk to me about my accounts. "If you took out a loan from the bank and prepaid the interest for five years," he said, "you could invest the money in real estate without paying taxes, because the interest is tax-deductible."

I followed his advice and proceeded to invest in local real estate. My first investment was in the City of Cypress on the corner of Walker and Ball Streets, where I built a shopping mall. I pre-paid the contractor, who flew to Mexico in his private plane, crashed, and subsequently died, leaving behind no insurance. In one swift act, I lost two million dollars. My second investment, however, was an apartment house on Orangethorpe Avenue in Fullerton, on which I *earned* two million. Experience was costly, but as Orange County real estate kept increasing astronomically at the time, I finished 1967 with a bang.

But my good fortune did not extend to the rest of the world. As the result of a March 1968 state-sponsored witch hunt, almost all of the Jews remaining in Poland were forced to leave the country. By the end of 1969, fewer than 10,000 Jews—some say as few as 5,000—were left in the country where I had been born, raised, hunted, and liberated. What the Nazis began, the Communists finished. A year later in Iraq, "... 9 innocent Jews were publicly hanged in Baghdad's so-called 'Liberation Square,' falsely accused of spying for Israel."[39] That same year in the USSR,

> Soviet authorities arrested a group of Jews in Leningrad who were attempting to steal a plane and fly it out of the Soviet Union. After a dramatic trial, they sentenced two of the hijackers to death—a sentence that was subsequently commuted because of world outcry. Then in 1972, with immigration beginning to increase, partly as a response to the protests of the Leningrad hijacking, the Soviets decided to implement a diploma tax, charging any Jew who emigrated an exorbitant fee, perceived as a kind of ransom charge, in order to pay back the Soviet education he had received.[40]

I counted my blessings to be in the United States of America, where Jews were no longer restricted by quotas or "Gentlemen's Agreements," and where a man could—with a lot of hard work and a little help from friends—rise to heights unfathomable to a little boy hiding in a dirt hole just twenty-five years earlier.

Both my medical practice and circle of influence continued to grow. Ron Rogers—the CEO of Bank of Newport, where I'd taken my original loan—became a good friend and asked me to join the bank's board of advisors. I did, and thus gained entrance into the inner circle of Orange County real estate. At one business function in the early seventies, I met Joan Irvine, the heiress of the vast Irvine Company, which owned virtually seventy percent of Orange County. From her I learned that the entire estate was available for $103 million. There were approximately four hundred physicians on staff at Hoag Hospital, and I arranged to speak to them at a meeting set up expressly for my purposes.

"I can arrange for each of us to get a loan of $250,000, and we can buy the Irvine Company outright," I told them. "The entire company."

My colleagues laughed me off the podium. Shortly thereafter, the Irvine Company transformed from a personal estate into a multi-million dollar corporation. By then, my colleagues had stopped laughing. But I had started thinking and planning.

While doing my fellowship at Sloan Kettering, I had become friendly with Dr. David Karnofsky and learned how he had arranged for Mr. Sloan and Mr. Kettering to finance the Institute. When he approached the two men—both of whom had at one time been chairman of General Motors—they informed him they were leaving shortly for Detroit, and that he'd have to accompany them on their private plane if he wanted to speak to them. He did, and they spent the trip questioning him as to why he deserved their support. When the plane landed, Dr. Karnofsky received a check for $100 million to create the cancer research center.

Remembering this story and my own experiences with the Rockefeller grant, I decided to create a foundation patterned on the Rockefeller and Ford organizations and set myself an objective of $1 billion to promote education worldwide. This goal soon took on the same fervor in the back of my mind as taking revenge on the Germans previously had. While not neglecting my oncology practice, I became increasingly active in business.

On Christmas evening, 1973, I was covering for my Christian colleagues so they could be with their families when I received a phone call from one of their patients in San Clemente. He was seriously ill and needed immediate attention, but no ambulance would take the call due to exceptional fog. They were right; I could barely see in front of my car as I drove to San Clemente myself. Eventually I pulled into a gas station to call the family and let them know I was completely lost in the fog. The wife asked for a description of where I had stopped and informed me I was merely one block from their house. When I got there, she helped me get him into my car; with her guidance, we drove him to the hospital, where I was able to attend to his desperate medical needs. He eventually recovered from his near-death experience.

A few months later, I received another phone call, this time from the man himself, who wanted to reward me for saving his life. He turned out to be the CEO of a major corporation that needed to dispose of some assets, and he was calling to offer me the opportunity to acquire them—and I only needed some nine million to do so. At that moment, I knew how my colleagues had felt the day I spoke to them about buying the Irvine Company. I, too, laughed at the prospect being offered; I had no such money.

"I'll loan you the money and you can make the acquisition. When you turn around and sell it yourself, you'll make a small fortune."

I took the deal, made the purchase, and he was right. When I later sold the property, I made a profit of $26 million. I realized that my dream of a foundation could indeed be turned into a reality, but I had to once again change my outlook—this time from medicine to real estate. So in 1977, I went to Colorado Springs, started looking around, and embarked on building my empire.

14

TREMENDOUS BUILDUP

1977-1986

As a result of my associations in both business and medicine, I got involved with politics, first on the state level, then on a national scale. I was such an active supporter of President Reagan, in fact, that I was invited to both of his inaugurations. In early 1983, after he and Gorbachev had verbally agreed that both the US and USSR needed to dismantle their nuclear arsenals and "stand shoulder to shoulder in telling other nations that they must eliminate their own nuclear weapons,"[41] the President inadvertently sabotaged that ambition by proposing the Strategic Defense Initiative to intercept and shoot down rockets. But while the "Star Wars" initiative was fated to fail for both political and technological reasons at the time of its development, I held considerable property in the area where the Air Force Planned to build its Consolidated Space Operations Center.

I had begun nosing around Colorado Springs in the late 1970s and established in rapid succession three companies: ML Properties, Inc., Centennial and Western Development Corporation, and List Enterprises. By the early 1980s, the potential in

Colorado Springs had become enormous; people were pouring into the area. With the Air Force's $1.15 billion, 640-acre Consolidated Space Operations Center (CSOC) now rising on the barren prairie just outside of Colorado Springs, a sort of space mania was sparked among the locals.[42]

> Dr. Martin List, who after a career in cancer research launched a real estate development business, dreams of creating an aerospace center on his 3,800 acres near CSOC. "I'm sitting on an empire," he says. "A whole city is coming up here. There's big bucks to be made here, and it's all about space."[43]

My plan was to build the Aerospace Center, a 3,800-acre commercial-industrial park that would provide jobs to some 40,000 people in twenty-seven million square feet of office space. I had set aside forty acres just for the construction of the List Institute for the Strategic Exploration of Space (LISES), my projected "think tank" of military and civilian scientists who would "address all issues relative to space, both military and civilian."[44] I was hoping to attract international scholars and promote synergism between the civilian and military defense organizations.

Yes, it was true: the lure of financial and political power combined with my zeal to create the List Foundation, and my total absorption in whatever work I had at hand—be it studies, medicine, or business—had driven me into a state of megalomania. I opened List Enterprises corporate offices in the List Building on List Drive. I developed housing tracts, shopping centers, and business offices. I surrounded myself with professionals and managed in a relatively short time to accumulate a vast fortune.

In due course I expanded into the neighboring states of Arizona and Oklahoma while still maintaining and increasing my business activities in California. In fact, I commuted almost daily between Colorado Springs and John Wayne Airport, because I still lived on the beach in China Cove, Corona del Mar. My neighbors there were wonderful and fun. One was Annie Hall, the mother of actress Diane Keaton, who at that time was living with Woody Allen and would later play the lead character in his most famous movie *Annie Hall*, named after my neighbor. Another was Marie Callender, whose pie business went on to become a national restaurant chain.

On weekends, I ran to my second home in La Quinta to recover in the serenity of the desert. I enjoyed the company of many beautiful and delightful women, but with a schedule like mine, I had no time for a relationship much less a marriage. I worked day and night—what woman would tolerate that? A newspaperman in Colorado once said, "You remind me of Lyndon Johnson. They used to tease him because he was always the last one to leave the White House at night. You're just like him: the last one to put out the lights."

Eventually, I even had my own bank. I bought the ailing Orange City Bank, changed its name to List American Bank, and moved it and List American Financial Inc. to Newport Beach. I even went so far as to establish my long-planned List Foundation in New York. These were heady times, made all the more so by my Who's Who list of friends and associates: Sam Walton, founder of Walmart; billionaire Sam Zell, largest shopping-mall owner in America; Arthur D. Little, founder of the world's oldest management consulting firm; world-renowned scientist Dr. Peter Glaser, inventor of the space solar power concept; then Texas Governor

John Connelly; Randolph Churchill, grandson of Winston Churchill; and numerous other powerful and famous people.

One of my good friends was Damian von Stauffenberg, CEO of Messerschmidt-Bölkow-Blohm (MBB), then the biggest industrial conglomerate in Germany. His uncle, General Claus von Stauffenberg, had been hanged from a meat hook for attempting to assassinate Hitler in 1944 by placing a bomb under his table. Damian once called me from Defense Secretary Casper Weinberger's office to ask that I show his crew around CSOC. Though it was still under construction and top secret, I had access through retired Air Force General James Hartinger, former commander of North American Defense Administration (NORAD), who was an employee of my corporations at the time. He immediately arranged permission for the Germans to see the site. They arrived with an army of media people and filmed everything I showed them—with General Hartinger's permission, of course.

About a week later, I received a phone call from a business friend of mine from New York who was visiting Berlin.

"Martin, I'm sitting here in my hotel watching German TV, and they're showing you and your doings in Colorado Springs!" Astrophysicist Peter Glaser was the advisor assigned to my project by the Arthur D. Little Co. A fellow Holocaust survivor from Czechoslovakia, he and I quickly became good friends. A few years earlier, the Organization of the Petroleum Exporting Companies (OPEC) had placed an oil embargo on the US, resulting in long lines and large price jumps at the gas pump, in an attempt to influence America's foreign policy against Israel.

This was also the time when people were becoming more aware of the "greenhouse effect" and the existence of acid rain.

Peter, an internationally recognized and respected scientist, advised me to construct a relay station on my Aerospace Center to transmit solar energy from the sun via the moon to feed America's need for clean energy. He calculated the project cost in 1985 at $200 billion. I could not fathom such an enormous sum.

I took the matter to another friend, Republican Bill Armstrong of Colorado, to whose campaigns I had previously donated considerable monies. I wanted him to introduce legislation to finance our solar-power madness, but I was unsuccessful. We were at a private dinner one night when I made yet another attempt to have him see the logic of our quest.

"Forget it," he said. "The Democrats are already screaming at the expense of the Star Wars concept. There's no chance of getting government money on such a scale for an unproven energy project."

Not to be deterred, Peter and I concocted a better idea. We organized a press conference in a major Paris hotel, and Peter and I jointly presented our plan to all the mega corporations of the industrial world from England, Europe, Japan, and the Soviet Union.

Unbeknownst to me, another friend of mine, Dr. Walter Purcell, who practiced in the same medical building where I'd had my offices next to Hoag Hospital, had brought his girlfriend to Paris on vacation and was staying in that same hotel. He noticed the press conference on the hotel's bulletin board listings, recognized my name, and walked in to watch the proceedings. I was of course delighted to see him, and we shared some champagne. Subsequently, all of Newport Beach heard about Peter's and my plans to solve the energy crisis.

Those were exhilarating times and I enjoyed them to the fullest. I felt I was doing important work, making a contribution to my adopted country and, by extension, to all mankind. Of course I was also profiting by my efforts, but I believed in the American ideal of reward for hard work. By the time I reached my apogee, I was mere inches away from having the net worth of the one billion I had set my sights on. And I had done it all in thirteen years—the same length of time Hitler was in power.

While I was reaching the lofty heights of my ambition, Jews were globally being cast once more as evil incarnate.

> …the Muslim world had little political concern with Jews until the period immediately preceding Jewish statehood. The establishment of the State of Israel in 1948 was a shocking, even a traumatic event, for it meant that at one stroke Jews had cast off their dhimmi status [second-class citizenship], conquered part of the Muslim patrimony, and made themselves rulers over Muslims. Christian power was bad enough, but to have Jews—the subject people par excellence—pushing Muslims around was too much. Muslims had to account both for their own devastating failure and for the Jews' unexpected power.[45]

This so-called new attitude of the Arabs toward the Jews—which in reality had originated approximately a century earlier but did not blossom until Hitler gave it legitimacy and impetus—gained enormous depth and breadth during the seventies and eighties while I was making my American fortune, thereby doubling my evil status in the eyes of disgruntled Palestinians and other anti-Capitalists.

A new theology of anti-Semitism and demonization of Jews has arisen. This theology was expressed most famously in the proceedings of the 1968 Al-Azhar Conference in Cairo and in the writings of the Egyptian Sayyid Qutb (d. 1966), which removed the ancient alleged Jewish distortion of Allah's initial revelation to them and the Jewish opposition to Muhammad from their legendary and historical contexts. Instead these two events were portrayed as describing an essential evil in Jewish nature.[46]

Saudi rulers had long connected Zionism with Communism, but the 1967 war intensified their anti-Semitism, and the ruling group that took over after King Faysal's death in 1974 stressed it even more than he had. The Saudis openly promoted anti-Semitism before any other Middle Eastern state; visiting foreign dignitaries were often presented with copies of the Protocols, and still are.[47] Copies were given away at the Consultative Assembly of the Council of Europe in Strasbourg. Faysal is reported personally to have subsidized the printing in Lebanon of 300,000 copies in a multitude of languages.[48]

The new anti-Semitism, which spread not only throughout the Muslim population but across a short-memoried Europe, cast Jews as fascists, imperialists, and malevolent conspirators trying to take over the world through vast, secret economic cabals. Though many of the verbal and physical attacks on Jews were carried out in the name of anti-Zionism, that epitaph merely lent a smokescreen of linguistic diversion from the perpetrator's underlying anti-Semitism; nevertheless, the results were unremarkably the same.

Admitting to being anti-Semitic after the Holocaust would immediately destroy one's credibility. Consequently, the new kind of anti-Semitism had to find another word than *Jew* for its propaganda. It chose *Zionist* or *Israel*, thereby throwing up a smoke screen. This trick has been successful as many have accepted that it is possible to be anti-Israel without being an anti-Semite.[49]

The turn to militant anti-Zionism had become unstoppable. From 1969 onwards the Palestine conflict was perceived purely as an integral part of the struggle of the oppressed peoples of the Third World against imperialism.

Already on 9th November 1969 – and the date had been consciously chosen – the "Black Rats/Tupamaros West Berlin", a forerunner of the "2nd June Movement", had struck their first "anti-Zionist" blow. They proudly announced in their statement of responsibility: "On the 31st anniversary of the fascist "Kristallnacht" several Jewish monuments in West Berlin were daubed with the slogans "Shalom and Napalm" and "El Fatah". In the Jewish Community Centre an incendiary device was planted. True anti-fascism is clear and simple solidarity with the fighting Fedayeen. For the Jews expelled by fascism have become fascists themselves, and, through collaboration with American capital, they want to eliminate the Palestinian people."

When a squad of the Palestinian organization "Black September" took the Israeli Olympics team hostage in 1972 – several people were killed when the police made an unsuccessful attempt to free them – the RAF (Red Army Fraction) expressed

> its enthusiasm for the exemplary character of this "anti-imperialist, anti-fascist and internationalist" action. Co-author of this document was Ulrike Meinhof – her biography is exemplary of the volte face of the New Left to blind anti-Zionism.
>
> In 1976 there was a further significant event: the highjacking of a plane to Entebbe by a squad of the Palestinian PFLP, supported by two members of the "Revolutionary Cells". In the plane "Revolutionary Cells" member Wilfried Bose organized the separation of the Jewish – and not just Israeli – passengers from the non-Jewish ones. Palestinians were to be released from Israeli prisons under the pressure of this hostage-taking of Jews. Even this horrendous event – recalling other practices when Jews had been selected – provoked virtually no reaction on the German Left. Anti-Zionism remained en vogue. [50]

It did not occur to me during these years that my own fortunes as a Jew were in any way related to these and other misperceptions and intolerances of my people. But I was an avid reader who kept up with global events, politics, and economics. I cannot discount the impact it had on my mental health when I realized the hatred that had destroyed my family, my community, and my childhood was not only strengthening throughout the Middle East, but again taking hold across Europe. Like most Holocaust survivors, I had put those years away, forced the memories into the dark recesses of my mind, and lived in the moment, for the future. I had focused and studied and worked and learned and made deals and arranged projects and enjoyed the luxuries of a life lived hard and fast. I was no longer the little Polish boy who was always hungry, the funny-speaking immigrant who was never good enough for the girl, the exhausted post-graduate trying to eke out a few hours of fun in a sea of work. I had climbed the mountain; I had made the grade. I was the embodiment of the American dream.

I should have known it would not last.

15

TERRIBLE BREAKDOWN

1986

As survivors age, they may experience a recrudescence of past symptoms, often activated by the loss of a loved one or a current stressor. Some survivors find it increasingly difficult to cope with traumatic memories and other symptoms such as nightmares, insomnia, and depression, as they become physically weaker. Many survivors have spent a lifetime trying to avoid dealing with the impact of the Holocaust on their lives and their families.[51]

The behaviors of survivors after their experience of the Holocaust can be classified in broad categories:

Death Imprint: A person is assaulted with death in such an intense way that the images are permanently burned into their mind. These memories are constantly on the mind of the victim and contribute to an intense realization of his or her own mortality (Kleber 98).

Survivors' Guilt: Why am I still alive when others have perished? Survivors guilt is connected primarily to the intense feeling of powerlessness experienced by the individual in the concentration camp. Also there is the concern on the part of survivors for their own lack of feeling while in the camp, i.e. anger, sadness and so on (Kleber 98).

Numbness: Used to explain the lack of or inability to experience emotions. It is a defense mechanism to avoid overwhelming memories, thoughts, and emotions, and in doing so creates a withdrawal between the victim and human contact (Kleber 98).

The Search for Meaning: Because of a survivor's continual confrontation with death and other atrocities during the camp experience, the survivor attempts to understand why these horrors happened to him or her, and the reasons behind these events (Kleber 99).[52]

At the point I came close to having $1 billion, I suffered a serious mental depression. With decreased energy to attend to my business, and with no family or intimate friends to support and help me protect my assets, some people around me cannibalized what I had so painstakingly created over thirteen-plus industrious years. Foremost among them was an Israeli family, the Nicheries, who I had the misfortune to meet—and in retrospect, the naïvité or extreme bad judgment of allowing them to work in my administration.

Unknown to me, the Nicheries had been convicted of over one hundred and thirty swindles, frauds, and thefts. Daniel Nicherie gained notoriety and pleaded guilty as a co-defendant in the wiretapping and racketeering case against Hollywood PI Anthony Pellicano. He has been in federal custody since 2004.

Taking advantage of my impaired health, they stole my identity, dismantled and sold off my life's work, destroyed my foundation dreams, and forced me into bankruptcy in January 1987. After that, my business acquaintances abandoned me, my homes were repossessed and sold off, and my every possession was taken away. I was left totally destitute without even a place to call home.

It is hard to describe what it's like to file bankruptcy after years of tremendous financial success. The very idea of the term only further aggravated my already serious depression. Just as people had previously flocked to me, they now abandoned me as if I had a contagious disease. As I signed the papers in the courthouse, I nearly fainted in my distress. The trustee who took over my estates had a final glance at my wrist.

"What kind of watch it that?"

"It's just an ordinary watch, a Timex," I said. "It's worth maybe fifteen dollars."

"No, you're lying," he said. "It's more expensive than that. I'll take it." As I handed over my simple Timex, he added, "Now get out of here, because everything you ever had is now mine."

I left the courthouse in a total daze. I was totally alone once again, without friends, without family, without any financial means whatsoever. The only thing I possessed was a ghastly sense of loss, failure, and contempt for my very life. It was unbearable.

Menachem, a friend from my childhood years, still lived in Israel. I managed to reach him by phone and describe my situation. Without a moment's delay, he provided me with a ticket to get on an airplane and return to Israel. I hadn't seen him in forty years, but he was waiting for me when I got off the plane at the Tel Aviv airport. He drove me to his home in Savyon, a somewhat swanky part of the city, where I was made to feel completely at home and part of his family. He also arranged for me to see a psychiatrist the next day. Though he gave me antidepressants, they did not help much.

I remained in Menachem's home for a number of weeks until I felt up to leaving on my own. I obtained room and board by becoming a house doctor at a Jerusalem hotel. I barely recognized the city for all the changes that had occurred since I defended it some forty years earlier. We had both changed, Jerusalem and I, but now I was back where I started—except I was fifty-eight, not eighteen. Poverty in youth is character building; in middle-age, it is character changing. My depression grew deeper with each beautiful Israeli sunrise.

One night, I could take the strain no longer. I went to a park and, like my grandfather all those decades ago, hanged myself. But unlike my grandfather, I was rescued in a timely manner. The weeks, months, and years following that aborted suicide attempt are now lost to me in a haze of psychiatric treatment and internal struggling to regain my footing in life. Eventually, I recovered—to some degree.

One day in October 1988, I decided to take a drive into the city center for lunch. I parked my little Peugeot in front of my favorite al Fresco restaurant in Jerusalem. As I headed back to my car after enjoying my lunch and reading my favorite newspaper, I spotted a sign on the building: "Lost Relatives Reunions."

My entire time in Israel at that point had been a series of recaptured memories, and the sign made me remember the little

Jewish girl I had rescued with the Russian sergeant who hated Poles even more than he hated Jews.

It was Friday after lunch, a time when all activities in Israel come to a screeching halt due to the imminent onset of Shabbat. The office secretary was preparing to close when I walked into the Reunions office and said, "There was this little girl I once handed over to the Jewish Agency. I would like to know where she was taken."

"What was the little girl's family name?"

"I don't know," I said.

The secretary burst out laughing. "You don't know? It's Friday afternoon, I'm about to lock up, and you want me to find someone whose name you don't know?"

I thought about it. "I know she had an aunt named Shonwetter."

The woman glanced at the clock and sighed. "Let me take a look." She brought out a shoebox with yellow cards in it. "Here are three Shonwetters. You can have the phone numbers of all three. Now go. Shabbat Shalom. Goodbye."

I took the numbers back to my hotel room and called the first one. The person who answered only spoke Yiddish, but she immediately knew who I was talking about.

"Yes, I know that story," she said. "That was my niece. She used to live here when she was married the first time. But when her husband died, she got remarried to a guy in Germany. She lives in Berlin now. Here's her phone number."

Ten minutes later, I talked to the girl I had rescued forty-two years prior. To my amazement, she recalled the details of the events just as I remembered them. She was now a happily married woman; her children and grandchildren all still lived in Israel on a kibbutz.

Hatred did not sleep while I fought my personal battles against old fears, new treachery, and mental anguish. Nineteen-eighty-eight saw the emergence of a new kind of anti-Semite: disgruntled and disenfranchised youth.

> There's one specifically dark cloud on the horizon," [Justin Finger, associate national director of the ADL] said, "the emergence of an import from England called the skinheads—young people in their teens and 20s who shave their heads into punk cuts, listen to hard rock music, wear Nazi regalia, and are bitterly hostile to Jews, blacks and Hispanics."[53]

Meanwhile, the First Intifada of the Palestinians against Israel ("officially" 1980–1991) gave birth to the extremist Hamas movement in 1987. "Hamas and Islamic Jihad initiated terror incidents and kidnapping of soldiers, and in fact, 1987 marked the coming out of Hamas as a terror group."[54] There were but a few years peace between the "end" of the First Intifada and the "beginning" of the Second Intifada, which continues to this day.

At the same time, anti-Semitism in the USSR was not only thriving, it was "government policy."

> No one should minimize the wide and deep traditional dislike of Jews among many Russians and Ukrainians which Mr. Morozov eloquently portrays. But decisions to exclude Jews from certain professions (the army, the secret police, the party apparatus) or to establish an organization like the Anti-Zionist Committee of Soviet Society are *policy decisions*, like how many missiles to

> deploy. They are made at a high political level, surely in some cases by the Politburo itself.
>
> Anti-Semitism was the core element, and perhaps the only clear element, in the jumbled Nazi ideology.... The Soviet Union is the only great state in history to finish a decisive victory over its greatest enemy by incorporating the core of the enemy's political program into its own politics.[55]

And while many people around the world did and continue to claim they are not anti-Semitic, merely anti-Israel, more than one study has concluded that being anti-Israeli or anti-Zionistic is really just an attempt to legitimize hating Jews.

After I recovered from my deep depression, I decided to return to Orange County, California, in October 1990. Fortunately, I was also able to recover considerable assets along the way, but I was nonetheless forced into retirement due to various ailments. I eventually had to undergo open-heart surgery due to a malfunctioning aortic valve and the need for a triple bypass. I was successfully resuscitated after the procedure but not quickly enough to prevent further complications. Lack of oxygen for four minutes combined with certain medications left my vision seriously impaired. Still, I managed to recover sufficiently to resume my intellectual activities—particularly reading, which was my favorite.

My recuperation from surgery, which included a tracheotomy, would have been impossible but for the invaluable support of a truly selfless friend, who devoted superhuman efforts to help me on at least three separate occasions.

Since my remarkable survival, yet again in the face of improbable odds, I have devoted myself to the study of historical and current anti-Semitism, for I believe that the world's treatment of the Jews has portended the great upheavals of societies throughout history. Those times when the Jews have been allowed to live quietly with their neighbors—an admittedly small percentage across the years—the world has been less dangerous and more inclined overall toward peace. Those times when the Jews have been persecuted—a much larger percentage of recorded history—the societies of the world have been more inclined toward war and destruction.

Recent events as of May 2009 indicate that the international community is at best indifferent to the fate of the offspring of the Holocaust survivors—Israel. Indeed I fear that once again there is an agenda by much of the world to sacrifice the remnants of our people for their own interests. I once believed that I had survived the worst that mankind had to offer: the horrors of the Holocaust and the devastations of criminal activity. Now I fear again, not just for my people—the Jews—but for all the peace-loving peoples of the world. Political correctness has become a disaster. It is time to finally face reality and to depoliticize evil. Regimes, ideologies, and policies that promote genocide and destruction are, in fact, evil and should not be perceived as anything but.

Perhaps it is true that Jews are the chosen people, but not for the reasons most often professed. Perhaps peace will not settle upon the earth until all the peoples of the world—most especially the Jews—are allowed to not merely exist, but thrive in comfort and security without fear of their neighbors or the stranger who comes amongst them.

But I know if this is to ever be the case, it will not be due to God's Will, but to Man's Will.

And so I worry.

AFTERWORD

Dr. Martin List passed away on August 23, 2010, in Mission Viejo, CA, after a sudden deterioration of his health. This memoir, which he wrote from 2006–2008, is a testament to a truly extraordinary human journey and a man who will never be forgotten.

NOTES

Chapter 1

1. "Hitler's Carmaker: As the Nazis Amassed Power, What Did GM Know and When? (Part 2)," Edwin Black. History News Network, http://hnn.us/articles/38255.html, accessed 7/31/07.

2. *No Haven for the Oppressed*, Saul Friedman. (Wayne State University Press, Detroit: MI, 1973). Accessed 7/31/07 on International Approach, http://teaching.arts.usyd.edu.au/history hsty3080/3rdYr3080/Callous% 20Bystanders/International.html.

3. "British White Paper of 1939," © 1996-2007 The Avalon Project at Yale Law School. The Lillian Goldman Law Library in Memory of Sol Goldman, New Haven, CT. http://www.yale.edu/lawweb/avalon/mideast/brwh1939.htm, accessed 8/17/08.

4. "Who was Harry Bingham and why is he getting a stamp?" Robert Kim Bingham, 12 June 2006. Free Republic, posted 13 June 2006. http://www.freerepublic.com/focus/f-news/1648645/posts, accessed 3/16/2007.

5. "1939: Germany invades Poland," On This Day, 1 September; video and audio from the BBC News Archive WWII and 1950-2005. http://news.bbc.co.uk/onthisday/hi/dates/stories/september/1/newsid_ 3506000/3506335.stm, accessed 8/3/07.

Chapter 2

6. "Babi Yar." Jewish Virtual Library: A Division of the American-Israeli Cooperative Enterprise. http://www.jewishvirtuallibrary.org/jsource/Holocaust/babiyar.html, accessed 8/6/08.

7. "Babi Yar," Yevgeni Yevtushenko, trans Benjamin Okopnik 10/96; http://remember.org/witness/babiyar.html, accessed 8/5/2008.

Chapter 3

8. "Memo Regarding Discussions at the Bermuda Conference (April 20, 1943)," British Foreign Secretary. Jewish Virtual Library, a Division of the American Israeli Cooperative Enterprise. http://www.jewishvirtuallibrary.org/jsource/Holocaust/bermudadiscuss.html, accessed 06/10/2006.

Chapter 4

9. "Bermuda Conference." Shoah Resource Center, the International School for Holocaust Studies. http://www1.yadvashem.org/search/index_search.html, accessed 8/14/2008.

10. "The Last Letter of Szmul Zygielbojm," Szmul Zygielbojm. Reprinted on The Home Page of Zigelboim, Krotman, Kamm and descendants Milnik, Finkelman, Buchstein; http://www.krotman.co.il/index-eng.htm, accessed 7/21/2008.

Chapter 5

11. "Slovakia The Legacy: The Tiso plaque controversy," Michael J Kopanic Jr. Central Europe Review, 20 Mar 2000, Vol 2, No. 11. http://www.ce-review.org/00/11/kopanic11.html, accessed 9/6/08.

12. "Kurt Waldheim's Knighthood, The Vatican, The Serbs and Israel," Manfred R. Lehmann. Manfred and Anne Lehmann Foundation, http://www.manfredlehmann.com/news/news_detail.cgi/128/0, accessed 6/11/2006.

13. "Croatia." Encyclopedia of the Holocaust, Vol. 1, p. 232. http://www.srpska-mreza.com/library/facts/ustashi.html, accessed 6/11/06.

14. "Kurt Waldheim's Knighthood."

15. "Genocide in Satellite Croatia 1941-1945," Prof. Edmond Paris. The American Institute for Balkan Affairs, ed. 1961, p. 132. http://emperorsclothes.com/docs/backin.htm, accessed 6/11/06.

Chapter 7

16. This incident was reenacted in the film *The Great Escape* based on the book by the same name, written by Luft Stalag III prisoner of war Paul Brickhill, an Australian fighter pilot.

Chapter 8

17. UNRWA Official Homepage (United Nations Relief and Works Agency for Palestine Refugees in the Near East); http://www.un.org/unrwa/english.html, accessed 10/6/2008.

18. "The Roman Ratlines: Early Efforts—Bishop Hudal," Wikipedia, http://en.wikipedia.org/wiki/Rat_line#cite_note-0, accessed 10/20/08; source Unholy Trinity: The Vatican, The Nazis, and the Swiss Bankers, Mark Aarons and John Loftus, (St Martin's Press 1991, revised 1998), p. 36.

19. "The Roman Ratlines," source Hudal Römische Tagebücher (English translation quoted in Aarons and Loftus, p. 37), http://en.wikipedia.org/wiki/Rat_line#cite_note-0, accessed 10/20/08.

20. Incidentally, no one is claiming a right of return to that area, or to Breslau (Wroclav) or the Sakhalin Islands, or the Sudentenland. Only the Palestinians feel they have a "right of return."

21. "British Mandate Anglo-American Committee," Palestine Facts, http://palestinefacts.org/pf_mandate_angloamerican_1945.php, accessed 10/20/08.

22. "The Bombing of the King David Hotel," Jewish Virtual Library, http://www.jewishvirtuallibrary.org/jsource/HistoryKing_David.html, accessed 10/12/08, quoting Menachem Begin, The Revolt, (NY: Nash Publishing, 1977), p. 224.

23. "The Kielce Pogrom," Bozena Szaynok, Jewish Virtual Library, http://www.jewishvirtuallibrary.org/jsource/Holocaust/Kielce.htm, accessed 10/12/08; Intermarium, Vol. 1, No. 3.

24. "The Bombing of the King David Hotel."

Chapter 10

25. "President Harry S. Truman and US Support for Israeli Statehood," MidEast Web Gateway, Ami Isseroff, MidEastWeb for Coexistence R.A., 2001-2003, http://www.mideastweb.org / us_supportforstate.htm, accessed 11/8/08.

26. "President Harry S. Truman and US Support for Israeli Statehood," Ami Isseroff.

Chapter 11

27. "Iraq 1950-1959: Nixon in Whitehouse. CIA Running Wild," Winston Smith, Never Fight a Land War in Asia, 2003, http:// www.secularsacrilege.info timeline/iraq 50s.jsp, accessed 11/14/08.

28. "Iraq 1950-1959," Smith.

Chapter 12

29. "Racism in the Middle East—Zionism or Arabism?" Ami Isseroff, e-Zion—The Zionism and Israel Viewpoints Online Magazine, http://www.zionism-israel.com/ezine/ Arab_Antisemitism_books.htm, accessed 11/18/08.

Chapter 13

30. "Palestine Liberation Organization (PLO)," Global Security.org: Military; http://www.globalsecurity.org/military/world/para/ plo.htm, accessed 11/29/08.

31. "The 1967 Six-Day War," Mitchell Bard, Jewish Virtual Library: A Division of the American-Israeli Cooperative Enterprise; http://www.jewishvirtuallibrary.org jsource/History/67_War.html, accessed 11/29/08.

32. *Battleground—Fact and Fantasy in Palestine*, Samuel Katz, Bantam Books, NY, 1985; pp. 10-11, 185; quoted in "The 1967 Six-Day War," Mitchell Bard.

33. "Correction by Khrushchev," *Time*, May 5, 1958; http://www.time.com/time/magazine/article 0,9171,863314,00.html?promoid=googlep, accessed 11/29/08.

34. "Soviet Jews under Khrushchev: Still the Total State," A. Wiseman and O. Pick, Commentarymagazine.com, Feb. 1959; http://www.commentarymagazine.com/viewarticle.cfm/soviet-jews-under-khrushchev-br-emstill-the-total-state-em-2963, accessed 11/29/08.

35. "Soviet Jewry in the Post-War Period," NCSJ: Advocates on behalf of Jews in Russia, Ukraine, the Baltic States & Eurasia; http://www.ncsj.org/AuxPages/history.shtml, accessed 11/29/08.

36. The Case for Israel, Isi Leibler, The Globe Press: Australia; 1972; quoted in "The 1967 Six-Day War," Mitchell Bard.

37. Leibler; "The 1967 Six-Day War," Mitchell Bard.

38. "A Catholic Timeline of Events Relating to Jews, Anti-Judaism, Antisemitism, and the Holocaust From the 3rd Century to the

Beginning of the Third Millennium," Jerry Darring, The Christian Heritage; http://www.sullivan-county.com/news/mine/timeline.htm, accessed 11/29/08.

39. "The Baghdad Hangings, Baghdad 1969: Iraqi Jewish Martyrs 30th Anniversary," Percey Gurgey, MBE; The Scribe, p. 29; http://www.dangoor.com/71page29.html, accessed 12/9/08.

40. "The Soviet Jewry Movement in America: The fight to liberate the Soviet Jews strengthened and united the American Jewish community," Gal Beckerman, MyJewishLearning.com, http: www.myjewishlearning.com/history_community /Modern/Overview_The_Story_19481980/America/AmericanSJmovement.htm, accessed 12/9/08.

Chapter 14

41. "Cold War to Star Wars," Jonathan Schell, *The Nation*, 28 Jun 2004; posted 10 Jun 2004 on http://www.thenation.com/doc/20040628/schell, accessed 12/8/08.

42. "Roger, Houston ... Er, Colorado," Richard Stengel, *Time*, posted to http://www.time.com/time/magazine/article/0,9171,1101850513-141721,00.html on 24 Jun 2001, accessed 12/8/08.

43. Ibid.

44. "Dr. Martin List: Physician Turned Developer Entrepreneur," *Who's Who in Colorado Springs, Real Estate West*, Feb, 1986.

45. "The Politics of Muslim Anti-Semitism," Daniel Pipes, danielpipes.org, 1981; http://www.danielpipes.org/article/161, accessed 12/9/08.

46. *Islamic Anti-Semitism in Historical Perspective*, Anti-Defamation League, 2002, pg. 3.

47. The Protocols of the Elders of Zion, an anti-Semitic tract alleging a Jewish and Freemason plot to achieve world domination, first published in 1903 in Russia to oppose the Communist revolution, but since touted in almost every language as proof of Jewish inherent evilness. The Protocols has been proven to be a fraud, and is "one of the best-known and most discussed examples of literary forgery." "A Hoax of Hate," Jewish Virtual Library, http://www. jewishvirtuallibrary.org/jsource/anti-semitism/hoax.html, accessed 12/10/08.

48. "The Politics of Muslim Anti-Semitism," Pipes.

49. "Anti-Semitism after the Holocaust – Also in Denmark," Arthur Arnheim, Jewish Political Studies Review, Fall, 2003, 15:3-4; http://www.jcpa.org/JCPA/Templates ShowPage.aspDBID=1&TMID=111&LNGID=1&FID=388&PID=0&IID=1104, accessed 12/8/08.

50. "Anti-Semitism on the Left," Thomas Haury, Workers Liberty: For international working class solidarity and socialism, 2006; http://www.workersliberty.org/node/6705, accessed 12/10/08.

Chapter 15

51. "Specialized Treatment Program for Holocaust Survivors and their Families," Traumatic Stress Studies Division: Specialized Clinics, Mount Sinai Medical Center, 2008; http://www.mssm.edu/psychiatry/tssp/holocaustsurvivor.shtml, accessed 12/11/08.

52. Lyn Williams-Keeler, Michael McCarrey, Anna B. Baranowsky, Marta Young, Sue Johnson-Douglas, "PTSD transmission: A review of secondary traumatization in Holocaust survivor families," Canadian Psychology 1998 (accessed on findarticles.com, Nov. 2005) http://www.findarticles.com/p/articles/mi_qa3711/is_199811/ai_ n8810928#continue; cited in "Do the Wounds Ever Heal? PTSD and Holocaust Survivors," Andy Douillard, for Prof. Marcuse's lecture course Interdisciplinary Perspectives on the Holocaust, UC Santa Barbara, Fall 2005; http://www.history.ucsb.edu/faculty/marcuse/classes/33d/projects/survivors/SurvivorPTSD_Andy05z.htm, accessed 12/11/08.

53. "Pn 02/11 1722 Anti-Semitism," The Associated Press, 1988; http://www.skepticfiles.org/nazi/antisem.htm, accessed 12/14/08.

54. "Intifada," Encyclopedia of the Middle East, MedEastWeb for Coexistence RA, 2007; http://www.mideastweb.org/Middle-East-Encyclopedia/intifada.htm, 12/14/08.

55. "Soviet Anti-Semitism," Charles H. Fairbanks, Jr., *Commentary*, commentary magazine.com, Dec 1988; http://www.commentarymagazine.com/viewarticle.cfm/soviet-anti-semitism-13741, accessed 12/14/08.

www.ingramcontent.com/pod-product-compliance
Lightning Source LLC
Chambersburg PA
CBHW020931090426
42736CB00010B/1105